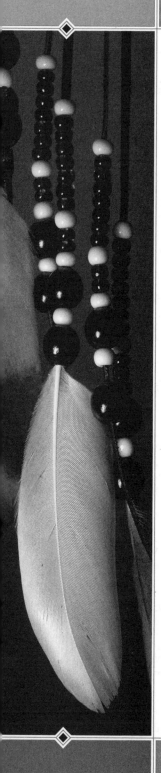

Native Elders
SHARING THEIR WISDOM

Kimberly Sigafus

Lyle Ernst

7th GENERATION

NATIVE VOICES
Summertown, Tennessee

Library of Congress Cataloging-in-Publication Data

Sigafus, Kim.
  Native elders : sharing their wisdom / Kim Sigafus, Lyle Ernst.
    p. cm.
  ISBN 978-0-9779183-6-2 (pbk.) — ISBN 978-1-939053-90-9 (e-book)
  1. Older Indians—North America—Biography 2. Older Indians—North America—
Attitudes. 3. Indian philosophy—North America I. Title.
  E98.A27S53 2014
  970.004'97—dc23

                                                                2013042440

PHOTO CREDITS

Ch. 1: courtesy of LaDonna Harris

Ch. 2: Carlos Puma for Dorothy Ramon Learning Center

Ch. 3: courtesy of Jacqueline Guest

Ch. 4: courtesy of Tr'ondëk Hwëch'in Archives, Michael Edwards Collection

Ch. 5: courtesy of Nella Heredia family

Ch. 6: courtesy of Jim Northrup

Ch. 7: courtesy of Judy Gingell

Ch. 8: courtesy of Christine Jack

Ch. 9: courtesy of Mark Bellcourt

Ch. 10: courtesy of Bert Crowfoot

Ch. 11: courtesy of Louva Dahozy family

Ch. 12: courtesy of Faith Davison

7th Generation,
an imprint of Book Publishing Company
PO Box 99
Summertown, TN 38483
888-260-8458
bookpubco.com

ISBN: 9780977918362

19 18 17 16 15 14   1 2 3 4 5 6 7 8

Book Publishing Co. is a member of Green Press Initiative. We chose to print this title on paper with postconsumer recycled content, processed without chlorine, which saved the following natural resources:

32 trees

938 pounds of solid waste

14,809 gallons of water

3,284 pounds of greenhouse gases

13 million BTU of total energy

For more information, visit greenpressinitiative.org.

Savings calculations thanks to the Environmental Defense Paper Calculator, edf.org/papercalculator.

D E D I C A T I O N

I t is with love and respect that this book is dedicated to those chosen for the title of "elder." It is our hope that with this book we will respectfully honor these special people. We are waiting for the wisdom only they can bestow upon us.

A C K N O W L E D G M E N T S

This book would not have been possible without the help of all of the wonderful elders included in it. They took the time to answer many e-mails, endured many questions, and ran up phone bills because they cared enough to call us back with the answers. We appreciate the grace the elders showed when accepting the invitation to be interviewed for this book, despite the fact that we were not always able to use traditional Native American and First Nation protocol when approaching them. This did not go unnoticed and unappreciated by us.

A big thank-you also goes out to Jody Beaumont, traditional knowledge specialist for the Tr'ondëk Hwëch'in. She was instrumental in interviewing Percy Henry.

Book Publishing Company editor Kathie Hanson also deserves a big thank-you. She was the captain of the Sigafus-Ernst boat and kept us on course throughout this process. Thank you for your patience and enduring faith in us.

C O N T E N T S

Native Elders

SHARING THEIR WISDOM

hen we think of the word "elder," some of us conjure up a mental image of an old person, wrinkly, slightly stooped over, and possibly a little cranky. While there is no doubt that such a person exists in some form in all of us, everyone comes with a unique story. Being an elder is more than just being old. Having taken journeys down paths that have taught them many things, elders pass meaningful and important lessons they've learned on to others. When elders speak to us about their lives, we are being gently taught. If we listen with our hearts as well as our ears, we can hear on many levels what is being said.

Elders are a precious resource in any nation. As one generation passes away, another group of elders moves up and into their positions. This is the cycle of life.

Each person's journey is very personal, and these personal journeys are what make every elder unique. The "Original People," whether they are First Nation or Native American, have very strong beliefs about where they have come from. Elders have stories to tell that have been passed down from generation to generation, as fairy tales and legends are. The difference between the two is that the elders' stories are a way of life for them. Some of the stories explain where their people came from, why things are the way they are, and what people can do to lead a good life. For example, living day to day we sometimes forget that we are not the only ones we need to think about. Because they have lived on the land for so long, the elders understand the need for everyone to work together to save the planet for future generations. They remind us that we are only borrowing the planet from our children, and someday we'll have to give it back.

In doing the interviews for this book, several recurring themes seemed to shine through: Protect our planet. Love those around us and treat them with respect. Young or old, everyone has a purpose and story to tell and deserves to be heard.

If the elders, or old ones, as they are sometimes called, are not respected and heard, our history will leave when they do. Without learning from our past, we can't confidently forge into the future. Without listening to those who have been around longer than we have, we lose our sense of where we came from and where we should be heading. The elders know it's their job to pass on the information they have learned. Our job is to listen. These are the reasons this book was written.

May the Four Winds guide us all.

LaDonna Harris

COMANCHE ELDER

Born in 1931 in Cotton County, Oklahoma, to a white man and a Comanche woman, LaDonna Vita Tabbytite Harris is one of the leading American Indian women activists in the United States. In Comanche, *tabbytite* means "sun rays coming through the clouds."

LaDonna was raised by her mother's parents, John and Wick-kie Tabbytite, on their 160-acre farm forty miles north of the Texas border, near the small town of Walters, Oklahoma. LaDonna's mother, Lilly Tabbytite, gave birth to LaDonna at home on the farm, not in a hospital. LaDonna's father was Lilly's second husband, a white man named Donald Crawford. Not long after her birth, LaDonna's parents divorced. Her father moved to California, and LaDonna only saw him a few times after that. LaDonna's sister, Billie, is from her mother's first marriage. With two small children to support, Lilly left her daughters with her parents and went to work at the Indian Health Service in Fort Sill, Oklahoma. She worked there for many years.

Billie and LaDonna had a wonderful childhood growing up on their grandparents' farm. There were always kids to play with because their grandparents enjoyed having young people around. The girls' cousins were always at the farm, and John and Wick-kie's daughter Rose Marie, who grew up on the farm, became like a sister to Billie and LaDonna. Wick-kie had a sewing machine and made everyone's clothes. "We were the best-dressed kids in school," says LaDonna.

Everyone called LaDonna's grandfather "Papa." He would braid his long hair with black yarn and always wore a big Stetson hat. LaDonna enjoyed helping Papa with chores like feeding the chickens, cattle, and horses. "Papa always had cattle, milk cows, horses, chickens, turkeys, and pigs," said LaDonna, "but no goats and no sheep, because he said they smelled bad."

Wick-kie had a big garden that she would plow in the spring with her horse. Later on, when Wick-kie became too old to plow, LaDonna would do it for her. Wick-kie would plant a lot of cantaloupes, watermelons, and cucumbers. LaDonna recalls that they would pick a cantaloupe early in the morning and put it in a wet dishpan with a gunny sack (burlap bag) over it. When they got done with the chores, Papa would get a big knife and slice up the cantaloupe. They would eat their fill, getting juice all over themselves, and then have fun pouring water on each other to clean up.

"I had great adventures," says LaDonna. She remembers that sometimes when she and her cousins were outside playing, they would watch rain clouds coming toward them. "In the summer we were always barefoot, and when we felt the first sprinkles, we would take off our clothes and run in the rain," says LaDonna. "Nothing smells so fresh and clean as rain hitting the dirt." After it quit raining, they would wash up in a nearby creek. The children played in that creek all summer long. North of the creek was the forest where they would go to get out of the hot sun. Every day as soon as breakfast was over, LaDonna and her cousins would run outside to play. At lunchtime, they would come in the house, make a bread-and-bacon sandwich, put some mustard on it, and go back outside. In the spring, there were lots of wild plums, grapes, raspberries, and blueberries for them to eat.

There was a big, old wood stove in the kitchen. When they wanted to iron clothes, they would heat metal irons on the stove. They didn't have running water in the house, but there was a sink with buckets of water sitting nearby. They would heat water on the stove for washing dishes.

Even though LaDonna grew up in rural Oklahoma during the Great Depression, her grandparents always had the latest things. Papa bought the first car in Cotton County, and he had a radio in the living room. Wick-kie had a wringer washing machine that sat on the back porch.

It was LaDonna's grandparents who instilled in her the values she has held throughout her life. They taught her that it's the Comanche way to trust and rely on your family and that everyone in a Comanche tribe feels related to everyone else. LaDonna learned a lot about life by keeping quiet and listening to adults as they talked. She always got along well with her aunts and uncles and loved them very much.

LaDonna Harris

Wick-kie was the second Comanche in the area to be converted to Christianity. LaDonna says the minister of the little church they attended and his wife were good white people who also farmed. The minister's wife even learned to play some Comanche songs on the organ so everyone could sing along. LaDonna and her grandparents would celebrate Christmas Eve and Christmas Day at the church, followed by Christmas at home, where the kids received gifts of oranges and candy.

Even though her family attended a Christian church, some of the worst discrimination in LaDonna's memory came from other ministers and churchgoers. LaDonna's grandmother taught her to feel sorry for those people because they knew nothing about the Comanche beliefs. It was better than getting angry. The best part of going to church was getting to be with relatives and friends.

When LaDonna was in high school, she was the only Indian in the school. She ran around with all the popular kids, and she joined school clubs and took part in many activities. She dated a lot and was allowed to do what she wanted without any strict guidelines. Her grandparents considered her old enough to be allowed to take a bus to Lawton to see her mother, and LaDonna would even stay with her sometimes.

By the time she turned sixteen, she had a steady boyfriend: Fred Harris, who was a student at the University of Oklahoma in Norman. They had met at a "juke joint" (a 1940s bar with a jukebox). Once they began going steady, they would meet at his parents' house, which was north of Lawton. During this time she was living with Aunt Rose Marie in an apartment in Walters, where she attended high school.

She would catch the bus to Lawton, and Fred would catch a bus or hitchhike from Norman to Lawton. LaDonna's mother would drive her from Lawton to Fred's parents' house. The two of them would spend weekends together going to movies or taking Fred's sisters to town.

Soon, they began going to dances at Fort Sill, where there were two or three big dance halls that had live music. Fred and LaDonna would be joined by her best friend, Floyce, Aunt Rose Marie and her boyfriend, and LaDonna's mother and her boyfriend. Sometimes they would stay overnight at LaDonna's sister Billie's house. Billie was married and lived in a Quonset hut. Sometimes the group would drive back to Lawton.

As her relationship with Fred became more serious, LaDonna decided she wanted to get married. Her mother and sister were against it. Her mother wanted her to be a model, and her sister didn't want her to marry a poor farm boy. But in 1949, right before high school let out, eighteen-year-old LaDonna married Fred Harris. She remembers the wedding fondly. "I wore a white suit and a little white hat. We got married in a little country church."

Fred went off with a harvesting crew to harvest wheat, because it was the fastest and best way for him to make some money at that time. They lived in Norman, and LaDonna went to work as a waitress. She recalls that he went as far north as South Dakota harvesting wheat.

After the birth of their first child, Kathryn, LaDonna got a job working as a hostess at the faculty club at the University of Oklahoma. Next, she went to work at the college library. She dearly loved that job. But the university did away with her position, so she went to work at the Center for Continuing Education. In this new job she was in charge of all the correspondence courses, which were offered to students via the US mail (similar to the way people today take college courses online).

During that time, the entire city of Norman was having a problem with rats. Fred, LaDonna, and baby Kathryn lived in a trailer house. LaDonna recalls reporting the rats to the housing authority and explaining that they had a baby in the house. The man she spoke with said, "Why don't you just feed them?" This horrible comment upset LaDonna.

Her sister, Billie, who was living in New Mexico, wanted to come see the baby. The first night she was there, a rat jumped onto her bed while she was sleeping. Billie screamed and Fred chased the rat around the house. The rat crawled into a cabinet and Fred couldn't get it. In time, the city of Norman got rid of the rat problem.

In the early 1950s, the family moved into a big, old house. They had hardly any furniture but managed to find a used couch for the living room. Fred was in law school and decided he wanted to go into politics. By now, he had made a lot of friends at the university, and they would all come over to Fred and LaDonna's house to discuss politics.

LaDonna recalls something from Fred's college years that made her feel bad when she found out about it—and what she did in an attempt to stand up for what she believed was right. When the university accepted its first black law student ever, the black student was required to sit behind a rope in the classroom. After another black student arrived, however, they did away with the rope.

The wives of the law students at the university gave Fred a scholarship because he was the top student in law school. They also put LaDonna in charge of the decoration committee for the fund-raiser dance.

Remembering the values that her grandparents instilled in her, LaDonna chose the black students' wives to be part of her committee. Some of the white wives urged LaDonna to take the black wives off the committee, but LaDonna refused. Instead, she made sure that the black couples sat at the head table with Fred and her.

Fred graduated from law school at the top of his class and joined a law firm in Lawton. During that time, he began to learn the Comanche language and sang Comanche songs in a Comanche church.

While living in Lawton, LaDonna lost a baby during birth. She was too depressed to go to the funeral. She and Fred had two more children: Byron was born in 1958, and Laura came along in 1961.

In 1956, Fred was elected to the Oklahoma Senate where he served until 1964. That year Fred ran for the United States Senate and won. During his term, Fred worked hard for Native Americans. He and LaDonna moved to Washington, DC, and were invited to all of the presidential parties and political events. In 1971, he unsuccessfully ran for president, with LaDonna campaigning by his side.

Throughout the 1960s, LaDonna was a suppor Native American causes. In 1970, she founded America for Indian Opportunity, headquartered in Albuquerque, New Mexico. She ran the organization for forty-two years.

LaDonna is a national leader and has positively influenced many organizations. She is a founding member of Common Cause and the National Urban Coalition and has worked with civil rights leaders, feminists, and environmentalists. She was also a founder of the National Women's Political Caucus, and in 1980 she ran as Barry Commoner's vice presidential running mate for the Citizens Party. She has worked for world peace and is a spokesperson against poverty and social injustice.

LaDonna Harris is a remarkable woman who has touched the lives of thousands of people. Even in her eighties, she is still a force to be reckoned with as she continues her work for world peace and social justice.

LaDonna Harris wearing a type of dress that is worn only by "Comanche Women of Distinction."

Ernest Siva

MORONGO ELDER

Born on February 7, 1937, Ernest Siva grew up in the 1940s and early 1950s on the Morongo Indian Reservation near Banning, California. The reservation covers thirty-five thousand acres and sits at the base of the San Gorgonio and San Jacinto Mountains, a few miles north of Palm Springs.

Ernest and his family lived in a one-room house that his grandfather built in the 1930s. There was no electricity in his home until the 1960s! Before that, they used kerosene lamps for lighting and a wood stove for heating and cooking. There was no indoor plumbing, which meant no toilet, so everyone used the outhouse. One thing they did have was a battery-operated radio that Ernest listened to as much as possible. He especially loved to listen to music.

Ernest said he remembers carrying the water his family needed into the house in buckets, which he filled from an outdoor water pipe that stuck out of the ground. They would heat the water on the stove to wash clothes in the bathtub. His mother used a scrub board for scrubbing clothes and heated a heavy metal iron on the stove to press the wrinkles out of shirts and dresses.

Children on the reservation rode the school bus to attend a public school a few miles away in the town of Banning.

Most of them took sack lunches. Ernest remembers that his older cousin, the first Siva to attend public school, once buried his lunch in the ground the same way a dog would bury a bone. He thought it would be safe there, but when he went to get it at lunchtime, the ants had beaten him to it. Ernest's cousin learned a valuable lesson: the school-room was a much safer place to keep his lunch!

Ernest Siva

Eating in the school cafeteria was a new experience for Ernest. There he had brown bread for the first time and learned that it is traditional to eat turkey and dressing on Thanksgiving Day. His family didn't eat turkey or chicken at home. His grandfather, Pete, didn't like turkey or chicken; he liked rabbit and deer, and since Grandpa Pete hunted rabbits a lot, that's what they ate.

Ernest enjoyed music from an early age. "I would sing when I was alone," he recalls. When he was in first grade and his cousin was in third grade, they sang the song "Grey Squirrel." Even today, more than six decades later, Ernest can still remember the words to that song.

Ernest remembers another song that he learned when he was very young—a lullaby that Grandpa Pete taught him when he was about four years old. Grandpa Pete and Ernest were sitting on the ground one day when Grandpa Pete suddenly started singing a song that Ernest had never heard before. It was called "The Dragonfly Song." As he sang, Ernest's grandfather made a motion with his hand over a rock where a dragonfly was sitting, and the dragonfly didn't fly away. Ernest reached over and made the same waving motion with his hand. Grandpa Pete told Ernest that the dragonfly was asleep, and that if a dragonfly doesn't fly away when you wave your hand above it, people say you'll have good luck. He also taught Ernest that the song he was singing attracts dragonflies.

Ernest recalls that his Aunt Julia loved to sing all kinds of songs—even "The Star-Spangled Banner." One of Ernest's favorite songs that she sang was "Ucha Tirvarc," a Morongo lullaby about a misbehaving bear. This is another song that has stuck with Ernest throughout his life, and he uses it as a learning aid when teaching Morongo vocabulary to students of all ages. The lullaby is also included in *Voices of the Flute*, a music book he wrote for a Native American flute class. The book, which was published in 2004 by Ushkana Press, includes a CD of Ernest playing the flute.

When he was around eleven or twelve years old, Ernest discovered some musical talent he wasn't aware he had. While listening to music on the radio, he heard an advertisement offering a harmonica and a songbook in exchange for a cereal box top and $1.98. Both Ernest and his cousin sent away for harmonicas, but only Ernest followed the instructions and learned to play.

In the seventh grade, Ernest took up playing the saxophone. The school provided musical instruments for students to borrow. Later, he received a scholarship to a summer music camp along with a friend who played the trumpet. The camp was conducted by the outstanding and well-known Idyllwild School of Music and Arts (now known as the Idyllwild Arts Academy), which was founded by Max Krone, the director of the Institute of the Arts at the University of Southern California.

This was a life-changing experience for Ernest. It gave him direction and helped him make decisions in his life that would have a major influence on his future. Competition at the school was fierce, which meant lots of practicing and studying. "I met many fine musicians, artists, and teachers and was very inspired by them," says Ernest.

He returned to the camp every summer to work at various jobs, from washing dishes in the cafeteria to serving as a camp counselor. He later became part of the faculty and taught choral music, guitar, and the Native American flute. He still plays the Native American flute today.

When Ernest was growing up, his mother always expected that he and his sister would go to college, so Ernest took college prep courses in high school. His mother often asked him if he wanted to be a University of California Los Angeles (UCLA) Bruin or a University of Southern California (USC) Trojan. She ingrained it in his mind that he would be one or the other, and it turned out that he became both. He attended USC, where he studied music and sang opera and, best of all, met his future wife, June. They both sang in the choir. He also played flute in the Trojan Marching Band. Later, early in his career, he taught courses in American Indian music at UCLA. Ernest says that both experiences were great.

His first teaching job was in a public school in Palm Springs, California, not very far from where he grew up. He taught vocal and general music. Ernest enjoyed it so much that it didn't seem like work. He taught the choir to sing in French, German, Italian, Spanish, and Latin. Ernest thought it was important for his students to learn to sing in foreign languages because great music comes from all over the world.

Ernest believes that his native language is also important. He is a member of the Morongo Band of Mission Indians, which is composed of a number of small groups of California Indians including Cahuilla, Cupeno, and Serrano. Each group has its own language, and each language is spoken within the western United States and Mexico.

Ernest speaks Serrano and is learning the Cahuilla language. In Serrano, Ernest's name is Termernc, which means "antelope." In the Cahuilla language, which Ernest's father spoke, the name Siva means "spring," as in a source of water.

Ernest's family's determination to keep their native language alive has been passed down for generations. Sometime around 1900, Francisco Morongo, Ernest's great-grandfather and a leader of the Morongo people, instructed his people on what they should do to keep their beliefs and their language. This was a time of great change, when many Indians were sent to live on reservations. Francisco told the people they would have to change their lives and learn the "new way" of living. They would have to learn the white man's language, but it was important to never forget their own language and where they came from. Keeping their language, he told them, would make them strong and give them deep roots like an oak tree's.

At one time, Serrano was spoken over a wide area of Southern California, but in the 1980s, it began to disappear. Ernest's aunt, Dorothy Ramon, a granddaughter of Francisco Morongo, remembered her grandfather's words and was determined to save their language. She understood that the history and traditions of the Serrano people are woven into the fabric of their language, and if the language was no longer spoken, their culture would disappear forever. She believed that her people's very identity was defined by their language. When she became an elder, she emphasized the importance of passing on traditional knowledge and remembering "who we are and where we came from."

Dorothy Ramon was the last person who thought, talked, and dreamed in the Serrano language first. "She truly was the last traditional Morongo," says Ernest. When she died in 2002, friends and family members agreed to carry on her work. Shortly thereafter, in 2003, Ernest, who is the Morongo Reservation tribal historian and cultural advisor, got together with other members of the Morongo and formed The Dorothy Ramon Learning Center in her honor.

The purpose of this nonprofit organization is to preserve and share American Indian cultural knowledge, now and for the future. "Our mission," says Ernest, "is to save and share cultures, languages, histories, music, and traditional arts of the Indians of Southern California."

Ernest points out that The Dorothy Ramon Learning Center is not a museum, does not collect artifacts, and does not focus on the past. It's all about the future. The center gathers information that might otherwise have been lost and keeps it accessible to future generations. Members of other tribes who wish to restore and revive their cultures seek Ernest's advice as an elder. "Traditional teachings have helped me all my life," says Ernest. He reminds us that these traditional teachings may seem simple, but following them takes effort. Here, in closing, Ernest offers some teachings that he considers very important, not only for young people, but for people of all ages:

Share knowledge, food, and aid of any kind with others.

Respect private property, ideas, beliefs, and customs.

Whatever belongs to another person (or people) should be left alone and not taken without permission or violated in any way.

Become good at doing one thing at a time.

Never stop learning and progressing in your knowledge, skills, and training.

Be open to new ideas and ways of doing things.

Be strong in your faith, and be loyal to your family and friends.

Always keep a positive attitude, and look for good in others.

Listen to your elders.

Jacqueline Guest

MÉTIS ELDER

J acqueline Guest is an award-winning author of historical fiction and a Métis elder. Her books have been nominated for awards in Canada and the United States, and she won the 2013 Indspire Award for the Arts. This Canadian award, formerly known as the National Aboriginal Achievement Award, is given to First Nation professionals who demonstrate extraordinary career achievement. They're given the award because they inspire others and are important role models for all First Nation peoples.

To Jacqueline, being an elder is important and should not be taken lightly. She wants young people to understand that it's crucial for them to have a deep connection to their heritage, something she feels is disappearing in our ever-changing world.

"Elders are a bridge to the past and a passport to the future," she says. "Through our stories, children come to understand the strength and stamina of our ancestors. If they weren't so tough, so strong, and so smart, we wouldn't be here today. We need to honor our ancestors. This important life lesson is communicated by today's elders who want to help our youngsters understand this."

Jacqueline also believes elders are here to help children achieve the success that is waiting for them if they try. "With our many years trailing behind us, we already know how hard one has to work to be a success," she says. "Nothing worthwhile comes easy, but it's always totally worth the effort. We can draw on our own life experiences to show that being a winner starts in your heart first."

When Jacqueline was a child, children were expected to be "seen and not heard." She wishes that she had asked more questions and requested more stories about the old days. She also wishes she had listened more closely to what her elders tried to pass on, because some of their knowledge disappeared when they passed away.

Born in the Turner Valley of Alberta, Canada, in 1952, Jacqueline has lived in a log cabin near the Kananaskis River in Alberta for the last twenty years. During that time, she's been chased across her deck by a

Jacqueline Guest

bear and used her Métis sash to lasso a blue jay that had gotten into her house.

"I may be old," she says, "but I'll tell you, when a full grown male bear is right behind you, your feet will grow wings!"

Jacqueline has become accustomed to being surrounded by animals. She shares her land with moose, deer, cougars, bobcats, rabbits, squirrels, skunks, foxes, and birds.

Her maiden name is Tourond, and she can trace her roots back to the days of the fur trade of the late eighteenth

Jacqueline Guest enjoys winter sports in Alberta, Canada.

and early nineteenth centuries. Joseph Tourond worked for the North West Company as a voyageur. He went on to work for the Hudson Bay Company as a middleman and, later, as a Freeman in the Red River area of Manitoba. Jacqueline's great-great-grandmother homesteaded at Batoche, Saskatchewan, where she and her family fought for Métis rights in the North West Rebellion against the Canadian government. She had two sons killed in the battle and another who died shortly after. Her house was burned down, her cattle were killed, and her horses, including a prized stallion, were stolen.

"My great-great-granny was no shrinking violet," says Jacqueline. "She was so incensed at these outrages that she marched across enemy lines and demanded they give her the stallion back! General Middleton was so dumbfounded that he gave her the horse and her buggy and sent her back home before resuming the battle."

Jacqueline's father, James Tourond, was a "Métis lad," as she puts it, from Pincher Creek, and her mother, Violet

Hocking, was Welsh. During World War II, Violet was a flight mechanic in the Royal Air Force and fixed Spitfire planes. In 1926, Jacqueline's grandmother, Rose Hocking, was a suffragette in Wales and fought for women's rights. Jacqueline believes that the influence of these strong women explains a lot about her approach to life.

"I've never backed down from a fight," she says.

Her father James and his brother Patrick served overseas during World War II. While stationed in England, James and Patrick Tourond met and married two sisters, Violet and Lorraine Hocking. After the war, both families returned to Black Diamond, Alberta, to live. Jacqueline has two older brothers and one younger sister.

"I guess it was a case of two handsome Canadian soldiers sweeping them off their feet," says Jacqueline, with a smile.

Jacqueline and her family moved around a lot when she was young. Her father was a truck driver who worked in the oil industry, so they went where the oil was. Jacqueline lived in several different towns along the route from Alberta to Saskatchewan and back. She spent the majority of her school years in Turner Valley, Alberta. Once she married, she moved to Calgary, where her two daughters were born. She has one grandson who is "the star at the center of my solar system," as she puts it.

There is no such thing as the perfect family, says Jacqueline. Everyone has problems of one kind or another, and Jacqueline's family was no exception.

"We cannot change the past, but we can shape the future into whatever we choose," she says. "I choose a bright future filled with love, laughter, and hope. I think my family will agree, if we all keep working at it, things will turn out just fine."

While she was growing up, Jacqueline didn't have a lot of friends. "I would rather spend my time reading than playing outside with worms and bugs," she says. By reading, she discovered what she says was a little secret: you can discover entirely new worlds through books.

Even though Jacqueline preferred reading books to spending time with kids her age, there was one person who was very special to her. Judy Poole lived not far from Jacqueline in Turner Valley. They went to high school together. She was a great friend and ally. Judy and Jacqueline did all kinds of things together and got into some trouble as well.

One Saturday, Judy agreed to let Jacqueline give her a home perm that came in a box. Jacqueline had never done this before but agreed to give it a try. Things were going fine at first, but when Jacqueline had half of the permanent solution on Judy's hair, a boy called her on the phone. While Jacqueline talked, the girls were giggling and trying to be cool, not thinking about Judy's hair. Judy kept interrupting to ask about one of the boy's friends, and Jacqueline was trying to be casual and not sound like it was the first time a boy had ever called her, which it was. Eventually they hung up the phone and finished the perm. Jacqueline doused Judy's hair with the chemical solution to make it curly and set the timer—totally forgetting that she had already put perm solution on one side of Judy's head before the phone rang.

"Judy's head was cooked within an inch of the hair's life," laughs Jacqueline. "Her hair stuck out like a wire scrub brush on steroids, and the other side . . . well, it just looked bad. We were afraid her hair might fall out, and some of it did break off. I have a picture of her," adds Jacqueline, "and she does not look happy."

Despite this—and the time when Jacqueline fed Judy's dog cookies on the bus—they still remain friends.

Jacqueline believes that life is like being in a boat on the ocean. The tides are moving in and out, storms come crashing down on us once in a while, and sometimes we have wonderfully tranquil, sunny days. What we must remember is that everything is always changing. The dark storms on the horizon now will move past us, and the bright, sunny

Jacqueline Guest at the site where the Metís, Cree, and Dakota First Nations first fought Canadian military troops.

days will follow. "Have faith in the universe," she says, "but first have faith in yourself. You are captain of your boat and you can ride out the storm."

One of her favorite quotes comes from Hannibal, a military commander from long ago who was well-known for his conquests against the Roman armies: "We will either find a way or make one." This saying reminds her to never give up, not on her dreams and not on herself.

Another of Jacqueline's favorite quotes comes from Christopher Robin, a familiar character that originated in author A. A. Milne's beloved Winnie-the-Pooh books. She tells this to children when she talks to them about their dreams, expectations, and the road ahead: "Promise me you'll always remember: you're braver than you believe, and stronger than you seem, and smarter than you think."

In Jacqueline's opinion, "Christopher Robin is as good and wise as the old Chinese teacher, Confucius."

Jacqueline's love of reading and books led her to write them. "My dream was to be a writer, but I thought authors came from fancy cities like Toronto or New York," she says. "I now know that writers come from everywhere—from little prairie towns in Alberta to pueblos in New Mexico to high-rise apartments in Los Angeles and Vancouver, BC."

Jacqueline believes that if you have a writer's heart, you can live your dream anywhere. All you need is imagination and the discipline to sit in front of a computer until the story is done. For her, being a writer has been a true test of her honesty with herself. "If the book is not written, if you can't find a publisher, if you quit because it's hard, there is no one to blame but you," she says.

An author of more than fifteen books, Jacqueline has created characters that come from different ethnic backgrounds, including Métis, and they all face common family issues. "Books open the mind to the possibility that there are other worlds, thoughts, opinions, and ideas out there that you know nothing about," she says.

That's precisely why Jacqueline has chosen to write. She says there is power in books, because wisdom comes from

As part of her school program on Métis culture, Jacqueline introduces students to Métis clothing.

Jacqueline brings Metís culture to school students.

reading. The journey to success starts the first time some-one opens a book and begins to read. "Books can save you," she explains. "Even if you don't like what's going on in the outside world, you know your heroes will save the day in the imaginary one between the covers of that favorite story."

In Jacqueline's opinion, the biggest battle we face now is helping children become better readers. She's traveled extensively to get the word out on how important this is, and she's led many workshops for children and adults on the subject. She's also spent many years trying to write inter-esting novels that will engage, entertain, and educate chil-dren. "If kids have great books," she says, "they will read. We simply need to keep offering them great books!"

Jacqueline feels that our electronic world has both very positive and very negative aspects. On the one hand, the Internet has made the retrieval of information on any topic available to everyone. This means we are able to access the world and learn about anything that piques our interest. However, this tidal wave of information can be overwhelming. As a result, young people now tend to have specialized knowledge about only things that interest them, rather than a shared base of common knowledge about many things. She feels that young people know everything about the latest skateboards but nothing about the countries that border their own. They can quote the latest rap music lyrics but have never heard of Tolstoy or Dickens. Broad-spectrum common knowledge is becoming lost.

"It's my hope that imagination doesn't fade out of the world," she says. "Imagination and curiosity are linked. When we imagine something, we become curious about it, which leads to investigation and increased knowledge."

Jacqueline believes that without imagination, there can be no advances. "If we can't imagine a better mousetrap, we can't build one," she says. "If we can't imagine the cure for cancer, we can't discover one."

She is convinced that children have the capacity to create a better world, not just a better city or community. However, in order for this to happen, we need to encourage young people to read and help them understand what they are reading. Reading leads to better grades, which improve kids' chances of going on to college. Children who read widely will, Jacqueline believes, grow into adults who might solve the world's food problems, bring about world peace, and find the cure for cancer.

Jacqueline understands that children face many difficult and sometimes frightening problems today. "To know they are not alone, that we are all in one big family who care about each other is important," she says. "We can communicate this message in many ways, but especially by giving our children role models and heroes who succeed."

"Life is a journey on a road that we build as we travel along it," she adds. "There will be bumps we need to smooth out, rocks we must climb over, and deep holes we will have to climb out of. It's worth it to reach our destination, to arrive at the life we have dreamed of, and know we did it ourselves."

Percy Henry

TR'ONDËK HWËCH'IN FIRST NATION ELDER

In my younger days, there was never such a thing as Indian Affairs or welfare. I never heard of those things because our welfare is the land.

—PERCY HENRY

Percy Henry is a Tr'ondëk Hwëch'in First Nation elder from Yukon, Canada. He was born in 1927 near the Ogilvie River and grew up in the Blackstone River region. Percy's parents raised him with traditional values, which he retained and upheld throughout his life, and which eventually helped him become a respected Tr'ondëk Hwëch'in elder.

Joe and Annie Henry, Percy's parents, taught their children the importance of living in harmony and balance with each other and the land. They spent the majority of their lives on the land hunting and trapping. Joe was a renowned snowshoe maker whose tools are now in the Dawson City Museum in Yukon, Canada. Annie was well-known for tanning hides and for her beadwork. Joe and Annie made history in 2000 when they were entered into *Guinness World Records* as the longest-married couple in history. They had been married for eighty-two years when Joe died in the spring of 2002 at 104 years old. Annie died in the fall of 2005, when she was 101 years old.

Percy Henry enjoys playing his violin.

When Percy's mother was growing up, she and her family spent the majority of their time traveling throughout the Northwest Territories and the Yukon. Most of their travels were by foot or dogsled team. She loved preparing fish and other meats, and she also liked to sew. She grew up speaking a dialect of the Gwich'in First Nation language called Takudh, which is still the church-worship language of many Gwich'in people. Her favorite book was her Bible, which was written in the Takudh language. She used to read the Bible to Percy regularly when he was young.

Joe Henry, Percy's father, was born in 1898 at the peak of the Gold Rush. He did a lot of trapping and hunting during his life, and he was one of the few men who knew how to make snowshoes, dogsleds, and ceremonial drums. He passed down these traditional skills and knowledge, in addition to his snowshoe-building technique, to his children and grandchildren.

Joe and Annie's marriage was arranged by their elders. They married on July 15, 1921, in the village of Moosehide in Yukon, Canada. Annie used to tell the story of how the two didn't even know they were going to get married until it happened! In those days, Tr'ondëk Hwëch'in young people didn't have a say about who or when they married.

Joe and Annie eventually had thirteen children and became grandparents and great-grandparents. The two traveled and lived off of the land their whole lives, never permanently residing anywhere. Although Percy's parents had thirteen children, only twelve of them lived to adulthood. Percy is the oldest of five brothers and six sisters. In 1935, Joe and Annie moved their family about three miles down the river from Dawson City to Moosehide Village, where Percy attended the Moosehide day school through the second grade. That's as far as his formal education went. For the rest of his life, his classroom was the land.

Percy's father instilled in him an exceptional work ethic. Percy spent time hunting and trapping with his father for many years. He eventually quit trapping because it was hard work for not much pay. The land was cold and harsh and he only made about fifty dollars a trip.

When he was twelve, Percy moved out of his family's home. He got a job as a fisherman's assistant and received only a dollar for every eighteen-hour day he worked. At the time, there were no gas boats, so Percy had to learn to use a poling boat (a flat-bottomed, shallow boat propelled with a pole) to check the fishnets along the Yukon River.

In 1950 Percy got a job at the sawmill in Mayo, Yukon, where he worked for nine years. During the winter, Percy worked as a cat skinner, a person who operates heavy logging equipment, for $1.50 per hour. In the summer, Percy worked on the *Brainstorm* riverboat hauling supplies between Dawson City and Old Crow. He then learned to operate the Campbell, McQuesten, and George Black ferryboats.

Percy Henry is a Tr'ondêk Hwêch'in language master.

Once he was proficient, he then trained new operators for the ferries.

Percy married his wife, Mabel, in 1958. They had eight children, but four of them died at a young age. Their living children are Mary, Selina, Liz, and Peter. Selina has given Percy and Mabel five grandchildren; she and her husband have four daughters and a son.

During the 1960s, Percy was a crew member for Yukon Highways and Public Works during the winters. He helped to maintain the Top of the World Highway for three years, and then went on to work for the rugged Dempster Highway, which leads to the Arctic Circle and beyond, for another three years. These roads are two of the most northerly highways in North America.

Percy is so respected in his First Nation that he was elected as their chief and served from 1968 to 1984. There was one period where he took a short break from his duties as a chief; during this time, he worked for Yukon Highways and Public Works operating heavy equipment and training ferryboat operators. Eventually, training ferry operators became his full-time job, which he did until 1980.

Percy takes his responsibilities as an elder very seriously. He feels that the wisdom he has gained from other elders and the lessons he has learned over the course of his life should be passed on to others.

"My purpose and responsibility at this time in my life is to speak up and to share truth as an elder and teacher sees it," he says. "An elder does not speak from opinions or theories but from personal experiences. When an elder uses passed-down knowledge, it is based on fact. It is certain after centuries of trial and error."

He admits that as a child it was sometimes hard to listen to elders who were trying to pass along words of wisdom to him. "I thought they sounded like a broken record," he says, with a laugh. But he believes children must keep listening to the words of their elders. Eventually they will come to understand what is being said and why.

Percy believes the old stories are important to pass on to future generations. If they are not told, they will die out, and no one will know them anymore. "Children can learn moral lessons from them," he says, "and the way to live properly."

The way you treat people, says Percy, is extremely important. "What goes around comes around," he states. "If you do someone wrong, you lose twice as much. If you give to somebody, it comes back twice as much."

Percy is extremely active in his community. It's very important to him that young people learn about their heritage. He's been working tirelessly over the past few years to have his knowledge recorded for future generations. Percy also spends a lot of time in his community's school, working with the children.

Recently, he joined the Tr'ondëk Hwëch'in Heritage Department staff as a language master. The Tr'ondëk Hwëch'in is a self-governing First Nation in Yukon, and this is a department within their government. Hän is the official language associated with the Tr'ondek Hwech'in nation. Percy is currently teaching a Tr'ondëk Hwëch'in language class. He is one of the last speakers of the traditional Hän language, one of several languages spoken in the Yukon. Only he and one other person in the world are fluent speakers of the Tr'ondëk Hwëch'in dialect.

His years as an elder have been very busy ones. He's worked as an elder representative with the Council of Yukon First Nations and with the Assembly of First Nations. He served as a member of the Yukon Geographical Place Names Board, and as a member of the Yukon Advisory Council on First Nation Child Welfare. He's also served as a member of the Dawson District Renewable Resources Council and as a strong advocate for language, heritage, and land programs.

Percy has been the recipient of many awards, including the Yukon Native Language Award, the Royal Canadian Mounted Police Award, and the Tr'ondëk Hwëch'in Elder of the Year Award. In 1999 he was ordained by the Anglican Church as the Reverend Deacon Percy Henry, and in 2002 he was awarded the Yukon Historical and Museums Association's Lifetime Achievement in Heritage Award. On June 21, 2002, Percy received a Commissioner of Yukon Commissioners' Award for his services as an elder and his many community-based activities and projects; he also received the first-ever Conservation Award presented by the Yukon Fish and Wildlife Management Board. In January 2005, Percy and his wife, Mabel, were named Mr. and Mrs. Yukon at the Yukon Sourdough Rendezvous, which has been held annually in Whitehorse, Yukon, since 1945.

Percy is committed to passing on everything he has learned during his lifetime, including the importance of the land to First Nations people. He has worked most of his adult life bringing attention to First Nations land claims and is committed to helping people understand why the land claims are important.

Percy Henry with Gramma Susie (Sharon Shorty, left) and Cache Creek Charlie (Duane Aucoin, right) celebrating the fortieth anniversary of the land-claims document Together Today for Our Children Tomorrow. Percy was one of the chiefs who created that document and presented it to Prime Minister Trudeau in Ottawa in 1973.

In 1977 he and several Yukon First Nation chiefs traveled to Ottawa, Ontario, the capital city of Canada, to present a document to Prime Minister Pierre Trudeau regarding First Nations land claims. Items such as gaining land ownership and the ability to self-govern were included in the document. The chiefs wanted the prime minister to understand their passion for First Nations land and the need for change in land claims. The prime minister took them very seriously, and the document became the basis for the Yukon Land Claims negotiation and settlement. Currently, eleven of the fourteen Yukon First Nations have been able to work out their land claims and tribal rights issues.

Percy is described by his friends as fun, funny, and full of life. He continues to live a traditional Tr'ondëk Hwëch'in life of

Percy Henry in Whitehorse, Yukon, on February 14, 2013, celebrating the fortieth anniversary of Together Today for Our Children Tomorrow with Tr'ondëk Hwëch'in Chief Ed Taylor.

hunting and fishing, but he also likes to try out new technology and is always interested in new ideas. Percy holds the Tr'ondëk Hwëch'in traditional way of life in great esteem and believes it's important to pass these traditions on to future generations.

"We all need to come together and walk together," he says. He admits that this is more difficult than before, as multiple generations of a family don't live together in a single dwelling like they used to. It was easy to pass on important things to young people while living in such close quarters.

Percy has seen many changes in his lifetime, but one thing he finds particularly alarming is the change in the weather. "The climate is changing," he says. "I've never seen weather like this." He believes Mother Earth has a shield around her, and it has holes in it now. He believes that people's negative thinking doesn't help the situation. "It's blocking out the sun," he says. "It can't heal [the holes] because of the negative thinking."

Another concern he has is for the fate of the earth. "We'd better take care of Mother Earth," he says, "because otherwise we're not going to leave anything behind."

In 2005 Percy gave a "Voice of an Elder" speech in Dawson City, Yukon. In his speech he told the audience his hopes for the present and the future. "Come together today, for tomorrow is too late," he said. "Let's all put aside our differences and put a purpose to our 'todays.' Let's stop being busy and start achieving results. Otherwise there is no 'tomorrow' for our children. Let's make every day 'today.' May the Four Winds guide us all."

Nella Heredia

CAHUILLA ELDER

Born in 1928 at the Soboda Indian Hospital on a southern California Indian reservation, Nella Heredia, whose birth name is Leonella, focuses on her belief in God when advising young people. As an elder, she works with troubled young people who have problems with drugs and alcohol. She emphasizes staying in school and getting an education.

Nella grew up listening to her father tell Bible stories and sing Native American songs at bedtime. The family of six boys and two girls was raised on the Pechanga Reservation in California's Temecula Valley. Her father, O. J. Salgado, grew up as a member of the Pechanga Band of Luiseño Indians. Her mother, Martha Arenas, grew up on the Cahuilla Reservation near Anza, California, where Nella is enrolled and now lives.

The family attended Sunday church services on a regular basis. Many times after the services, the pastor, who was American Indian, would come to their home with his family for lunch.

When Nella's parents first married, they lived in a house near the Pechanga Reservation. In the early 1930s the Bureau of Indian Affairs (BIA) began setting aside twenty- and ten-acre lots for members of the Pechanga Band. Later they built houses on those lots. While their new home was being built, Nella's father built a ramada, a house made out of willow poles and branches from small trees and shrubs.

The family lived in that house for about ten months. It had a room to put a dining table in and a kitchen with a wood-stove to cook on. The kitchen also had a cupboard, a break-fast table, and one large room where the family slept. The boys slept on one side of the room and the girls on the other; the parents slept in the middle. Nella loved that house because it was cozy, and she didn't want to move into the new one.

Nella Heredia

After they moved into their new home on the BIA acreage, Nella's father became a farmer who raised chickens and hogs. He also had a team of mules for plowing the garden. All the children were responsible for feeding the animals in the mornings and the evenings. They helped pick vegetables and fruits from the garden, and the girls helped their mother with canning food for the winter. They also helped with the dishes.

Nella recalls her mother's meals. "They were the best," she says. There would be homemade buns, stews, tortillas, and pies and cakes for dessert. Her mother also cooked rabbit stew and mustard greens. "We had to sit up straight at the table," says Nella. "Elbows off the table, and we had real cloth napkins."

Nella says her parents were very giving people. Once the family moved into their new house, any person in need who came around was helped. Nella's parents taught Nella and her siblings to respect other people and never let anyone go away hungry or in trouble.

The most fun she remembers as a child is the whole family traveling every weekend in the summer to different reservations for Fiesta, which included Native American dancing, horse racing, and rodeos. The young ones enjoyed a singing competition called Peon. It called for eight singers, four women and four men. A large bonfire was built and the women sat on one side of the fire, with the men on the other side. One person was a referee who acted as a judge. The men would kneel down and sing, and then the women would sing. Nella's brothers won the championship five years in a row.

Nella began school in the first grade. It was a one-room classroom with twelve students from first through eighth grade. The students were all Native children from the Pechanga Reservation, except the teacher's daughter, who was white. All of the students liked the teacher very much. She took them on a trip to the zoo and to see the ocean. Many of the friends Nella made going to that one-room school are still her friends today.

The next year the small school was combined with the Temecula Grammar School, located in the city of Temecula. Nella didn't like the school because there were more than twenty students in her class, which was many more than she was used to. The resulting culture shock became difficult for Nella to handle. She failed second grade and had to repeat it. The long bus ride to and from school was one big reason that she failed: she had to catch the bus at 6:30 a.m. and did not arrive at the bus stop closest to her house until around 5:00 p.m. Then, she had to wait an hour for her father to come home from work and pick her up at the bus stop. This left her little time for studying and doing her homework. Nella enjoyed her second year at Temecula, but because of the terrible commute, Nella switched schools.

Her parents arranged for her to live with family friends in Lake Elsinore, California. They had a daughter one year younger than Nella. After her sophomore year at Lake Elsinore High School, she transferred to San Jacinto High School, where she graduated in 1946. She loved San Jacinto High and played basketball and soccer there. Most of all, she got to go to the junior and senior proms. "I wore my first fancy dress that my parents bought me," says Nella. She took typing and shorthand in high school, hoping to land a job as a secretary. She also took three years of homemaking classes because she dreamed of one day owning her own restaurant.

After high school graduation, Nella went to work for Erle Stanley Gardner, a famous writer of mystery stories. Mr. Gardner owned a large ranch near the reservation where Nella grew up. She worked for him for a few years, both as a proofreader and as part of the waitstaff when famous guests came to dine with Mr. Gardner.

After graduating from a beautician college, Nella spent the next eighteen years working as a beautician. During that time, she also managed four beauty shops in San Bernadino, Hemet, and Escondido. She liked the job because she could schedule her own hours and her customers were very friendly.

In addition to working full-time, Nella was also raising her seven children—one son and six daughters. Today she has seven grandsons, five granddaughters, nine great-grandsons, and four great-granddaughters.

In 1971 Nella's longtime dream came true. She opened a coffee shop in a bowling alley. It lasted five years. It was in this environment that Nella realized people were not always friendly and in a good mood. She found this disappointing, but her little shop, named The Coffee Shop, was so successful that soon she began catering breakfasts and luncheons for businesses nearby. This led to a full-time catering business that is still thriving today. "Catering is almost always a happy time," says Nella. "People are having fun and are nice to get along with."

The name of her business is J.A.M.E.S. Catering. Nella asked her daughters to come up with a name, and they chose the initials of the first names of five of her grandsons. In later years, her daughters took over the business, but

Nella still helps out with cooking and delivering food for tribal meetings and celebrations on the reservation. The most popular item on the menu is tamales, which her daughter has been making for years. "Everybody chips in to help, including the grandchildren," she says.

Something else Nella enjoys is attending powwows, where she sells fry-bread with her daughters and grandchildren. Her favorite part of the powwow is seeing old friends again.

Nella has lived on the reservation for thirty-eight years. She is a member of the Cahuilla Cultural Committee, which continues to stress their cultural identity.

Eleven years ago, Nella's family, along with a family friend, started a Christian ministry called Cahuilla Native Lighthouse Ministries. Once each year the ministry holds a women's retreat offering counsel and information on various agencies and programs to women who need help. They assist women who live both on and off the reservation. The ministry has also proven to be extremely helpful to many young Indians who have problems with drugs and alcohol.

Nella says, "I talk to kids all the time. I tell them, 'Go forward with your knowledge. Life is completely different out of school.'" She tells them to make good decisions, to know who their friends are, and to know what direction they are going.

She has success stories to tell. One girl she took under her wing has gone back to school and is happy that she did. A young boy she gave advice to has gotten his GED. One of her favorite success stories involves a young man on the San Manuel Reservation, which is north of the Pechanga near San Bernardino, California. He works with young people and contacted Nella, asking her for help in prayer. She went to his reservation to meet him and join him in prayer. Since then, he has told her that things are better and many of the problems are gone.

Nella enjoys working with young people and will continue to do so until she is no longer able.

Jim Northrup

ANISHINAABE/OJIBWE ELDER

Boozhoo aaniin ezhi-ayaayan niijii is the Ojibwe phrase for "Hello, how are you, friend?" Meet Jim Northrup, an Anishinaabe/Ojibwe award-winning author, journalist, poet, and playwright, as well as a loving father and grandfather. Jim lives with his wife, Pat, in the tiny unincorporated community of Sawyer, Minnesota, which sits on the Fond du Lac Reservation near Duluth. As an elder, he believes it is essential that all Indigenous people preserve their native languages.

In fact, Jim is so dedicated to preserving the Ojibwe language that he and Pat have run Ojibwe language immersion camps for the last three years. The camps are held at a campground near Sawyer and are not only for children; entire families, including grandparents, attend. "The first year," says Jim, "we had 189 people come." In 2012 there were more than 500.

Jim Northrup signs a copy of his book, *Rez Salute: The Real Healer Dealer.*

Many of the adults who attend the language camps have grown up either speaking or surrounded by speakers of their native language, but no longer use it. All they have to do is locate their memories of Ojibwe and bring them back. Others come to camp to learn the language without ever having heard it before.

But Jim believes that "our language defines who we are." And with everyone working together, Native languages can be preserved. "This," says Jim, "is the main goal of the language camp," and it's the cause to which he has made a lifelong commitment.

Along with the yearly language camp, Jim holds Ojibwe language classes every Thursday night at the community center in Cloquet, a small town on the reservation near Sawyer. During the first hour of each class, Ojibwe is the only language spoken. Jim also teaches his native language in the course of his daily life, such as when he teaches his grandchildren how to count in Ojibwe. He says that the most important advice he can give children is to "learn your language, and listen to the old stories."

The oldest son in a family of ten brothers and sisters, Jim was born in a government hospital on the Fond du Lac Reservation. At the tender age of six, he was taken to a federal residential boarding school in Pipestone, Minnesota. He was there for four years. "They were not fun years," says Jim. "I learned how to fight, because crying didn't stop the beatings."

Jim was not the only child beaten at the boarding school. He remembers that the nights were the worst. A young kid would start crying in his bed, and pretty soon everyone in the room was crying. Beatings and loneliness were what he remembers. He even tried running away, but he was caught.

Other than those four years, Jim spent the rest of his childhood growing up on the reservation. Many of his memories are unhappy; like many Indians, he had to put up with racism and prejudice. Also, his father was an alcoholic, which did not make life easy.

RESIDENTIAL BOARDING SCHOOLS

The residential, or boarding, school system in Canada was founded in the 1800s. By 1884, education outside the home became compulsory for Aboriginal children under the age of sixteen. If parents refused to send their children to school, they risked facing time in prison.

The United States opened residential boarding schools for Indian children about the same time as Canada. The schools in the United States were first set up by Christian missionaries, but the US Bureau of Indian Affairs was established in 1824 and opened additional boarding schools.

Both in the United States and Canada, the schools forced the assimilation of Indian children into white society. Indian students' long hair was cut off, they were not allowed to speak their Native language, and they could not practice religious ceremonies. Many students suffered physical and emotional abuse at the hands of their teachers.

The Canadian government closed the last First Nation residential school in 1996. All the large Indian residential schools in the United States have also been closed, although a few small schools remain in operation.

The biggest changes in Jim's life occurred during the 1960s. After graduating from high school, Jim joined the United States Marine Corps. Many members of his family had joined the military before him. He was an infantry soldier, and his unit was constantly training for combat. During the Cuban missile crisis in October 1962, Jim's unit was on a ship sitting offshore from Cuba. Nothing ultimately happened to require their service, so his unit was sent to Puerto Rico to practice more war games. His unit also traveled to Hong Kong,

Jim Northrup

the Philippines, Taiwan, and Okinawa, Japan. "Everywhere I traveled," says Jim, "people would come up to me and point at my hair, skin, or eyes and say 'same-same.'"

Jim continued training for war and rose to the rank of corporal. After thirteen months in the numerous countries of the Far East, Jim returned to California, where his military career had begun, and became a military policeman at Barstow, California. While he was stationed in Barstow, the Marines landed in Vietnam. At that time Jim extended his enlistment so he would have enough time for a thirteen-month tour of duty in Vietnam. He was sent to Vietnam with the Third Marine Division, where he participated in combat against the Vietcong. He was promoted to sergeant, and while on patrol he accidentally stepped on a land mine that, thankfully, failed to explode. After his thirteen-month tour, he was awarded an honorable discharge from the US Marines.

After returning stateside and working in various factories for a year, Jim became a deputy sheriff back home in

Carlton County, Minnesota, where parts of the Fond du Lac Reservation are located. After some years he transferred to the Waukegan, Illinois, police department. He stayed in

Jim Northrup

that job for several more years before going to work as a security officer at a nearby college. From there he joined a public defender's office as an investigator working on the defenses of those charged with serious crimes like murder and robbery. Jim didn't like working with criminals, and after some time he left and returned to the reservation. This was in the mid-1970s.

Housing and jobs were scarce when Jim came back home, so he lived in a tipi for about six years. Finally, he was able to get a decent-paying job in construction, and in 1983 he moved into the house he lives in now. By then he was writing short stories and starting to get published. Jim has since published four books, with two more scheduled to come out in 2013. He has won numerous honors and awards for his writing, and he is especially proud of the honorary degree he received from Fond du Lac Tribal and Community College in Cloquet, Minnesota, a doctorate of letters—the first one ever awarded by that institution. For the last twenty-three years, Jim has been writing a monthly column called "Fond du Lac Follies," which appears in several newspapers. In his column he mixes humor, political commentary, and observations about life on the reservation. Jim writes mostly because he enjoys it and feels that his contributions—sharing an Anishinaabe perspective and showing what life is like for his tribe—are important.

Jim and his wife, Pat, a Dakota from the Lower Sioux Indian Community in southern Minnesota, have been married since 1986. Together, they have eight children, many grandchildren, and one great-grandchild. They live according to the seasons in Sawyer. In the spring, Jim and his sons fish for walleyes and northern pike, and in the summer, Jim makes birchbark baskets to sell. He learned how to make the baskets from his grandfather. Pat, who is also a Jingle Dress dancer, makes moccasins. In the fall, the family harvests wild rice for food and the boys hunt moose and deer. In the winter, Jim's sons

Jim Northrup making a birchbark basket.

tap maple trees for making syrup, just as he taught them. Jim does most of his writing in the winter.

Jim says that the best piece of advice he can offer to young people is to "treat others like this is your last day on earth."

Judy Gingell

KWANLIN DÜN FIRST NATION ELDER

Not too many people have experienced riding on a dogsled, and of those who have, few took their first ride as infants. But Judy Gingell did! Judy was born in 1946 in a small cabin near Moose Lake, which is located in the Yukon Territory of Canada, about two hundred miles south of Whitehorse. Her parents, John and Annie Smith, lived out in the wilderness and helped Grandpa Smith take care of his line of animal traps. Annie and John had traveled to a cabin closer to other people for the birth of their baby, but they couldn't stay away from the traps for too long. So, as soon as her mother was able, Judy's father packed his wife and newborn baby girl on his dogsled for the trip back to the main cabin where they lived.

Years later, she recalls her dad saying that it was really, really cold the day she was born. He told her he could hear the trees cracking. Baby Judy was all bundled up in furs. In order to be sure she was okay, her dad would reach down and pinch her nose, after which she would move around.

A member of the Raven Clan of the Tagish Kwan, Judy grew up in Whitehorse and has lived her entire life there. She is the eldest of ten siblings, nine girls and one boy. Her sisters are Shirley, Dianne, Edith, Betsy, Kathy, and Rosemarie, along with Lesley and Alice, who are deceased. John is her brother. "We all are best friends," she says with pride. "When someone is in need, our family is there for them. Growing up, we took care of young nieces and nephews. All of us would go out into the wild with our grandparents, where we would gather berries and roots used for medicine."

"I enjoyed spending time out on the land hunting and fishing," says Judy. In the summer, the family would live with Grandpa and Grandma Smith, camping out in tents and living in a cabin. "We would load everything on the truck except the kitchen sink."

"Those were the good old days," says Judy. "My mother enjoyed living off the land and camping."

In the late 1800s and early 1900s, the government of Canada established a program for educating Canada's Aboriginal people. Called "residential schools," they were run by

Judy Gingell

the the Department of Indian Affairs and Northern Development (now known as Aboriginal Affairs and Northern Development Canada). The Indians had no choice; it was mandatory that their children attend the government-run schools. The government hired agents to make certain that all Aboriginal children joined a residential school.

Once the children were in school, they were prohibited from speaking their own language and practicing Native traditions. They were no longer allowed to wear Native clothes. Brothers and sisters at the same school were separated because boys and girls were not allowed to mix. The living conditions in these schools were awful, and students were mentally and physically abused.

In 1951 Judy and her sister Shirley were taken from their home and forced to attend the Whitehorse Baptist residential school. They were only allowed to come home during the summer and for a Christmas break. Judy's sisters Diane, Edith, and Lesley were taken to the residential school at Carcross, Yukon, located south of Whitehorse, close to the border of British Columbia.

Judy vividly recalls the terrible manner in which she was treated at the mission school. The children were beaten if they spoke their native language. The teachers called them "Indian people" and told them they were no good and would never amount to anything. "The teachers made me feel so bad that I was ashamed to be an Indian."

When asked what dreams she had as a child, Judy answered, "My dream should have been to complete high school. But because of the strict rules, the mistreatment, and too much religion, I only had one dream: to get out of that school."

Judy was happy when she was told that she could leave the school when she turned sixteen, so she jumped at the chance. Her first job was babysitting, and even though she only had a ninth-grade education, she entered the Yukon Vocational and Technical Training Centre (now Yukon College) to become a bookkeeper. Judy says, "I have benefited from that training my entire life. It has helped me understand financial systems and how to communicate with others who may not have the same training."

Judy says the best advice she can give to young people is "get an education and be prepared." She says, "Most of what I have learned so far is through experience and hard work. I continue to expand my knowledge. Education is important."

In 1968 Judy, along with other Yukon First Nation leaders, founded the Yukon Native Brotherhood. The association was formed to allow the First Nations the right to be heard and work at convincing the government of Canada to recognize their rights. Judy was appointed secretary/ treasurer. That same year she became the manager of the Whitehorse Indian Band, which is now known as the Kwanlin Dün First Nation.

Judy, along with other chiefs and leaders, became a dedicated and powerful force who was a leader in claiming land settlements for her people and pushing for political change in the Yukon. She is widely regarded as one of the most influential political figures in the territory.

Judy tells young people, "Read our people's history so you can understand where you are today. Be proud of your people and yourself. Be accountable and responsible for your actions in a good way. Let your heart guide you, and be grateful."

In 1973 the First Nations began a long struggle to convince the Canadian government to settle their Aboriginal land claims. Judy traveled with Yukon First Nation chiefs, elders, and community leaders to Ottawa, the capital of Canada, where they presented a statement of grievances to Prime Minister Pierre Trudeau. That statement, titled "Together Today for Our Children Tomorrow," became the foundation of the Yukon Land Claims.

Judy's father also traveled to Ottawa, as he was the chief of the Whitehorse Band, a position he was elected to four times. In earlier years, Judy's grandfather had held the position of chief.

Judy Gingell holding "The Order of Canada," her country's highest civilian honor, awarded "for her years of service in various Yukon Aboriginal organizations."

In 1974 Judy became a member of the Yukon Indian Women's Association (YIWA, now called the Yukon Aboriginal Women's Council, or YAWC), and in 1977 she was appointed to serve as the association's vice president. It was this group of determined women from all across Canada that pressured the government to pass Bill C-31 in 1986, which amended the Indian Act of 1876 and, among other things, gave Native women more rights.

Before Bill C-31 was passed, when a Native woman married a man from a tribe other than her own, she gave up her tribe and automatically became a member of her husband's tribe. If an Indian woman married a non-Native man, she lost her tribal status altogether. Because Judy married a non-Indian man before Bill C-31 was passed, the Canadian government took away her status as a First Nation woman. After that she was no longer registered as an Indian and could not be a member of a First Nation band. Getting Bill C-31 approved was vitally important to Judy and other First Nation women who married non-Indians.

The Yukon Indian Women's Association was also active in putting a stop to the use of First Nation cemeteries as tourist attractions. This practice was not merely perceived as disrespectful; some tourists—they were driven through the cemeteries by the busload—would steal Indian works of art, such as small statues. At that time, the Canadian government printed tourism brochures that included maps for locating First Nation cemeteries. The women of the YIWA protested and demonstrated against this, and eventually, the government took the cemetery maps out of its brochures. It was then that the association raised money to place signs outside of the cemeteries instructing tourists not to enter.

In 1989, Judy, at the age of forty-three, was elected chairperson of the Council for Yukon Indians. She served two consecutive three-year terms. She was appointed to the second term because, when her first term expired, the council was at the stage of finalizing the self-government agreement and needed members who had been involved in the process from the beginning. Judy and the vice-chairperson headed the general assembly comprised of sixty-five members. More than twenty years after the founding of the Yukon Native Brotherhood, self-government for the majority of Yukon First Nations was finalized in 1993.

After serving in numerous leadership positions, in 1995 Judy was appointed by Jean Chrétien, then the prime minister of Canada, to serve as the Commissioner of Yukon. She was the first Aboriginal person and only the second woman to serve in the position since it was established in 1897. This was the first time she represented all of her people. She says that working in a non-Aboriginal world was different, but she enjoyed it. Judy held the position until the year 2000.

One of the commissioner's duties is hosting the annual Commissioner's Ball in Dawson City, Yukon, each year. The ball honors the gold rush era, a time when lace and fine clothes were worn by the people who became rich from finding gold. Through the years, very few First Nations people were invited to the Commissioner's Ball. Judy was determined to include her people in the tradition. Indians had been displaced by the gold rush, and Judy could not allow her office and title to not represent her own people. Not only did she include First Nations elders, but she had fancy horse-drawn carriages pick them up from their hotel rooms and deliver them to the ball. One elder exclaimed that she felt just like a queen.

Judy's father taught her to care for the people she represented and to want only the best for them. He told her to be a visionary leader, imagine new possibilities, and trust in people and consult with them.

Her mother taught her to work hard, to not give up too quickly, to respect elders, and to never be lazy. She also taught Judy to think carefully before making decisions.

In 2010 the Canadian government appointed Judy a member of the Order of Canada, which is one of the country's highest honors and "recognizes a lifetime of outstanding achievement, dedication to the community, and service to the nation" (from the website of the Governor General of Canada, http://www.gg.ca). Judy's appointment came with thanks and appreciation for her more than forty years of work promoting and advancing First Nations rights in the Yukon Territory.

Presently, among her many other duties, Judy is executive elder of the Kwanlin Dün First Nations Elders Council. The Elders Council gives advice and guidance to the Kwanlin Dün First Nation about programs and services that meet the needs of elders. It also takes part in settling disputes. By appointing elders to sit on committees, the council also helps to preserve and protect Kwanlin Dün First Nation traditions, customs, and laws.

"Retirement" is not a word you'll find in Judy Gingell's vocabulary. "I can't retire," she says. "There is too much to be done."

Judy and her husband, Don, are parents of two children, Rick and Tina. They have three grandchildren (Kailen and Cameron Gingell, and Mackenzie Curtis) and three step-grandchildren (Ariel, Brittney, and David Curtis). Ariel presented her grandparents with their first great-grandchild, Ryleigh. Judy adores her grandchildren. She says she loves her children dearly, but her love of her grandchildren is different. "I can't describe it. They are precious jewels. I thank the Creator."

Christine Jack

XWISTEN FIRST NATION ELDER

C hristine Jack, who considers herself to be a deeply spiritual person, is a Xwisten tribal elder who lives in Lillooet, British Columbia, Canada. As a sweat lodge keeper for her people, Christine drums and sings traditional songs, seeks to pass on everything she has learned, and hopes to inspire others to be the best they can be.

"An elder, to me, is someone who has gained knowledge throughout their life through their experiences," says Christine, "whether good or bad, hard or gifted. An elder is one who shares, teaches, and passes on knowledge to others. They are honorable and humble to not seek to gain anything, but to be enriched from the experience and therefore enrich others."

Born on June 7, 1967, in Lytton, British Columbia, Christine Lucille Thom is her mother's tenth child and her father's fourth. She is the youngest of twelve children, three of whom died before Christine was born. Her two oldest sisters died in a vehicle accident when they were in their teens, and another sister died at the age of three.

Christine's father was a logger who also worked at other jobs, and Christine cannot remember her mother—who was an alcoholic in chronic ill health—ever having a job outside their home. Her father drank as well, and the family always struggled to make ends meet.

When Christine was young, her family didn't have running water or electricity in their home. Her earliest memories are of the chores she and her siblings had to do. Everyday life was filled with cooking and cleaning. As she looks back, she believes these were the times that gave her the good memories of her past.

Christine's father was not part of her everyday life. He lived an hour away in Lillooet, and she would occasionally visit in order to spend time with him. "I not only loved my father, but I liked him," she says. "He had many stories of hunting and fishing to share, and in those stories were always lessons to learn from." Christine says he was a soft-spoken man with a very strong work ethic.

Christine and her father had a very open and honest relationship, which gave her a good foundation on which to build as she later began to heal from the traumas of her youth. However, she felt that his drinking and living away from the family had negatively affected her. When she would ask questions about the past, he tried his best to be truthful, even when the answers were not easy for her to hear. "I would like to think that he knew the painful truth was going to give me the best chance to heal," says Christine, "and not just added poison to stop growing so I can hide in the pain." Christine was so grateful for the knowledge he gave her. Her father eventually passed away from bone marrow cancer in 1998 at the age of sixty-seven.

When Christine was seven years old, her mother's health was declining, so Christine and her youngest brother, Ralph, were sent to St. George's Indian Residential School, which was right across the river from their home. She was following in her family's tradition, since her grandparents, parents, and all but one sibling attended residential schools. When it was discovered that their mother was dying, she and her brother were allowed to go home and spend the last few months with her. Christine was only eight years old.

Christine Jack drumming while on a spiritual journey to the ancient Machu Picchu site in Peru.

Christine experienced what she considers the biggest loss of her life when her mother died of liver failure due to alcoholism. Life would never be the same for her. Both Christine and her brother Ralph had a difficult time dealing with their mother's death. They became very angry and started to act out.

All of Christine's siblings had left home by this time, so when her mother died, she and Ralph were sent to live with their aunt and uncle, Mary and Ed Napoleon, in Lillooet, BC.

She and her brother were put into a public school. She was called names and was bullied by the other kids. To make matters worse, when she was in the residential school, all of her hair had been cut off, so she looked like a boy. Life was not easy "for the little Indian girl," she recalls.

To hide the fact that she was lonely, hurt, and afraid, Christine started picking on other students. Even though she was only five feet tall, she could still hurt people when she was angry. Her ability to use words to hurt others became her preferred weapon. She would also pretend to be sick as a way of not dealing with her feelings—or with others' feelings. As she grew older she eventually realized that her anger was a result of the abuse she endured at the residential school she had attended.

She and her brother Ralph were very close when they were growing up. "He taught me to sing songs at the age of six," recalls Christine. "I remember him asking me to sing into a pillow so I could hear my voice and get over my insecurity." Aunt Mary and Uncle Ed taught Ralph and Christine traditional songs and dances; they were forming a traditional singing group and asked Christine and Ralph to be part of it. Christine remembers that their aunt and uncle also taught them the value of earning money. They earned the money needed for a new dance outfit, and if someone gave them something, they were told that that person had seen good things in them or was impressed by how they held themselves. When this happened it would increase Christine's confidence.

Christine feels that good, moral values were not taught to all children when she was growing up. However, even though her mother was gone, Christine still tried to live in a way that would show her mother what a good person she was. As she got older, though, the absence of her mother remained intensely painful. Despite her knowledge that her mother's alcoholism led to her death, Christine started to drink to escape her pain.

Her aunt and uncle took in several other children, most of whom had also lost their parents, during the time Christine and her brother lived with them. Eventually there were eight children in the house where Christine grew up. She was the second youngest at the time. It was at this point she met her best friend, Dee Dee Doss. She was the first person who didn't question her about being different or looking and acting like a boy.

It was also during this time she realized that living with such a large extended family would not be easy. She quickly figured out that the other kids would lie, steal, run away, and drink. They were always in trouble, and Christine decided she should be the one who would always tell the truth.

When Dee Dee and Christine were in high school, they started learning and performing traditional dances and songs. This activity kept them out of trouble. Christine found her classes in school to be fairly easy, but because she was an Indian, her teachers told her that she would not be placed in the more advanced classes. Eventually Christine became involved in sports, realizing that if she joined in sports activities, she would build herself up physically and mentally and she'd make new friends as well. Organized sports became her outlet. She played basketball, soccer, and floor hockey.

Christine graduated from high school in 1985, the first girl in her family to do so. Unfortunately her success in school was not enough to keep her from drinking. Christine and all of her siblings had struggles with alcohol and drug addiction. Two of her brothers committed suicide.

Growing up poor and Native, being enrolled in a residential school system that took her from her family, dealing with racism even as a young child, having alcoholic parents, and watching her mother die when she was only eight years old all led Christine to her alcoholism. At times, she has had to pull herself away from her family in order to give herself the best opportunities to heal. She's been to three

Christine Jack picking berries near her home in British Columbia, Canada.

treatment centers and numerous workshops and has gone to many traditional healers. She gained her sobriety when she was twenty-three years old. When she was thirty years old, she thought she could control her drinking but started doing drugs for two years. She ended up back in treatment and was sober and drug-free for two more years. Then her youngest brother committed suicide in her home. She went back to drugs and alcohol for another year. Eventually she realized she was on the same path as her brother, so she put herself back in treatment. Now she has ten years of sobriety to celebrate.

Even while dealing with her alcohol problems, after high school, Christine took a college course on office procedures, and she now has many certificates from other courses she has taken on topics such as anger management, life skills, boundaries, and emotional intelligence. She's also completed a leadership course and several classes on the subject of personal development. Christine now does personal empowerment workshops that are based on her personal healing journey.

Christine married Gasper Jack from the Xwisten First Nation when she was eighteen. They were together for seven years and then divorced. He is still one of her best friends, and because they agreed on the shared responsibility of raising their daughter, he has always been part of her every-day life.

Her family loves animals. They have always had at least one dog, and at one time they had five rescue dogs. They now have just one, and his name is Bud. He is fourteen years old, and Christine still feels like they got the pick of the litter.

Christine now has two daughters: Candice F. M. Jack, who is twenty-seven years old, and Alicia L. M. Jack, who is twenty-four. Alicia goes by one of her Indian names, Badger.

"These two women are the greatest people I know today," says Christine, "very strong, vibrant young leaders and teach-ers. I am so grateful they are also my friends. They are such a wonderful asset to the world."

Christine doesn't have grandchildren yet, but she certain-ly looks forward to that time in her life. She knows she will make a wonderful grandmother when the time comes. Chris-tine says that her Aunt Mary, who is now eighty-six years old, has been a great role model of how to hold yourself and share thoughts in a peaceful yet powerful way.

Today, only six of Christine's siblings are still living. They are not as close as they once were, but that's because they are all changing and healing at different rates. "I love my fam-ily and all the steps of hardship, celebrations, and triumphs that I endured to be who I am today," she says. "I'm very hon-ored and proud that I can offer the world a view of healing and transform my path into one that gives me respect, love, and trust."

She has many plans for the future, all of which help define who she is. "I moved here to Lillooet as a small child,"

PIT HOUSE

A pit house is a house that is made by digging a large hole in the ground that is big enough to fit the number of people who are to live in the house. Next, a flat roof made of mud-covered poles is built to cover the hole. The entrance is a ladder that's lowered into the house through a hole in the roof. Fires are built in the center of the pit house floor for light and warmth in the colder months. Pit houses don't last forever, though. Most of them have to be abandoned after ten years.

says Christine, "and stayed here on the Xwisten reserve for the last twenty-five years. In that time, I paid off my house and now plan to build a small, domed, earthbag-style home. Then I'm going to rebuild my pit house, which is one of our traditional homes. This sustainable building, as well as gardening, hunting, and fishing, are the things that get most of my time and attention. This is who I am. Whatever dreams I may chase in life, I continue to take care of myself as much as possible. I can dream and create this part of my life with joy and excitement."

Because of everything she has experienced, Christine feels that she has a lot of good advice to share with the youth who are growing up in the world today.

"You may be dealt many hardships in life, may it be through where you live, or through cultural injustice, poverty, or what family may expect of you," she says. "Through my experiences I have learned that being honest is one thing, but more so you should be honest with your feelings and thoughts. Trust that you're made in goodness. That's where a powerful purpose lies."

Christine believes that the most important part of her life has been her spiritual journey. "I gave myself an honest and worthy effort to heal from the events that happened to me, and therefore I'm a powerful, spiritual person today."

She believes in educating yourself to be all the things you may feel you lack—don't look outside of yourself for a leader. "When you come up against things that bring you fear, embrace your intuition. Learn to trust that voice that tells you things like 'walk away,'" she says. "When you know that you're around people or things that may hurt you, this voice is coming from the essence of your goodness."

Christine believes that there are many good people who truly care, and that we should surround ourselves with them. She also knows it's up to us to allow ourselves the opportunity to live life differently. "What is not working for us," she says, "is only a choice away from changing. I found when I let go of how other people would like me to be, and stood strong in how I'm meant to be, the more I would grow and change in a healthy way."

Life doesn't have to be painful, she says; it can be good, healthy, and exciting. "That's what I choose," she says. "Therefore I fit right where I am. I know I live a good life, and so can you. Be all you can, for the world needs you in your goodness."

Christine's journey has had many ups and downs, but she believes that each step was necessary to help her arrive at this place and time. "I am healthy, happy, strong, and gentle," she says, "but most of all I'm free to be me."

Christine believes that the world is headed into the greatest time of change. She says that as we awaken to our purposes, we will bring forth the change needed for a better world. "It is the children of the now," she says, "who are the most powerful people I like to walk with and the greatest teachers we have at this time. Therefore, free yourself from carrying forth any more historical pain, grief, or hatred. Create the peace we all seek; it is our turn and our time to be fearless. Be big. Be yourself. I once may have only been seen as an alcoholic Indian, or a victim of the past, but now I'm a powerful First Nation woman. I'm gifted in spirituality and ready to help others in their healing journeys by staying faithful to mine."

Mark Bellcourt

OJIBWE ELDER

Mark Bellcourt is an Ojibwe elder, an experienced traveler, and a teacher. He has degrees in education and counseling from the University of Minnesota and has worked extensively with Native American students.

Mark was born and raised in Nora Springs, Iowa. A small north-central town, it was filled with white people who were mostly retired farmers or children of farmers. Mark's parents were divorced before he was born, and he was raised by his mother, whose grandparents emigrated from England.

Mark's family lived close to the Shell Rock River, and a creek ran through their backyard. He was always playing around the water—even though three teenagers drowned in the river during Mark's childhood, that didn't stop him from loving the water. He was also curious about plants and animals.

Mark Bellcourt

59

Mark Bellcourt near Anchorage, Alaska.

He had three older brothers; one recently passed away. The other two are married with their own families. Mark's father was an abusive person and was absent for most of Mark's childhood. There were times when his mother had to protect the boys from their father during his infrequent appearances. Fortunately, Mark's mother had a very good relationship with his father's sister, Aunt Olie, and with Mark's maternal grandmother. They saw them often.

Mark's mother always told her children that they were not Native people. Mark had no reason to doubt her. She often told him to stop asking about his Native side and that he should just be white and try to fit in with everyone else. However, at age fifteen, he realized that if his grandmother, aunt, and father were Indian, then he must be Indian as well. It was a cultural awakening for him.

He and his brothers struggled in school. Mark says that being the youngest was sometimes hard because he had his brothers' school reputations to deal with. Every year on the first day of school, the teachers would do a roll call. When they came to Mark's name, they would often say, "Oh no, not another Bellcourt!" None of Mark's brothers graduated from high school, and at times it looked as though he would follow in their footsteps. Fortunately, his eleventh-grade art teacher recognized Mark's talent and encouraged him to go to college. Mark took his art teacher's advice. Even though he had to repeat many of his classes, Mark finally graduated high school.

As a child, he only had a few people he could call friends. Growing up in a poor, single-parent household was hard. He didn't have nice clothes and wore mostly hand-me-downs or second-hand items from Goodwill. Sometimes his family didn't even have money for food.

"I could never go to father-and-son events," remembers Mark, "or have money for school field trips, going out to a movie, or to get birthday or Christmas gifts. Our family was sort of looked down upon or pitied by my peers and their families." But Mark knew that no matter how bad things got, there were others who were even more impoverished or had harder lives than his.

When Mark was about eleven years old, he had an experience that left him confused. He was approached by one of his older brother's friends who wanted to be Mark's "special friend." "He never forced himself upon me," says Mark, "but certainly talked me into doing many sexual activities with him. Mostly just hugging, kissing, and fondling. I wasn't old enough to really understand sex yet. I just remember how nice it felt to be touched by another person." The friend eventually moved away and the relationship ended.

When it came time to start exploring his own sexuality, Mark was still really confused. Nothing felt right or satisfying. But at the time when Mark was a teenager, the prevailing cul-

Mark Bellcourt and his students near Hasting, New Zealand, during a class on Indigenous environmental knowledge.

tural attitude about homosexuality was extremely negative, so he was ashamed and felt he could never tell anyone about the sexual experiences he had had with the older boy. Because of the confusion caused by his early experience, and because Mark believed that being gay wasn't a "normal" option, he despaired that he would never have a happy, healthy romantic life. He thought he would never get married or have kids, and that he'd have to sneak around for unsatisfying, impersonal sexual encounters. He thought he was broken.

"I think feeling 'broken' is very common with survivors of sexual abuse, rape, and incest," Mark says. "I'm not sure if it entirely goes away, and certain events, activities, or conversations can trigger repressed feelings." Nearly everyone has some difficulty navigating dating and relationships, but sorting out your sexual feelings while also attempting to cope with abuse of any kind is particularly challenging.

However, after counseling and education, Mark now feels that he has resolved the turmoil of his teen years. "I have accepted and become the person I am with no regrets," he says. "I learned that I was not broken, just gay." He's been in a monogamous same-sex relationship for more than thirty-four years now.

As an adult, Mark is happy and confident in his identity, but his path might have been easier if he had felt he could talk to a trusted adult about what happened with his brother's friend. It is important to remember that if an adult or older person asks you to keep a secret that makes you uncomfortable—or if an adult does something inappropriate—then you should tell someone. An older person should not be doing anything to you or with you that should need to be hidden. "Don't be afraid to talk about your concerns and feelings," says Mark.

As a young child Mark dreamed of becoming a fireman or a doctor. But during his later teenage years, he wanted to become a protester and hippie and live in a commune somewhere in peace and harmony. But after the Vietnam War ended, civil protests were not as common and the age of "flower power" and hippies was not as inspiring to Mark, so he decided to go to college. It was there that he discovered his passion for education, and he feels that he's never stopped learning since. Mark's now a senior academic advisor at the University of Minnesota.

Mark's interest in his Native heritage came about as a result of two family members who in 1968 started the American Indian Movement, also known as AIM. Vernon and Clyde Bellecourt founded AIM for the purpose of addressing important issues, such as police brutality against Native Americans, and to establish the National Indian Health Board, which was the first Native American urban-based health care provider. They also worked on ways to combat the poverty that was being experienced by many urban Native communities.

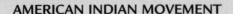

AMERICAN INDIAN MOVEMENT

The American Indian Movement (AIM) was founded in 1968. The focus of AIM is to guide Indian people toward a renewal of spirituality and impart the strength needed to reverse the disastrous government policies for Indians. Since it was formed, AIM has established many programs and organizations that serve Native Americans and Aboriginal people. AIM has returned to Indians millions of acres of land taken by the US government. The movement is still going strong today and continues to serve its people well.

Vernon and Clyde Bellecourt's family and Mark Bellcourt's family descend from two Bellecourt brothers who came to Minnesota from Canada back in the early 1800s. The family has three different spellings for their name: Bellcourt, Bellecourt, and Belcourt. Vernon and Clyde are the sons of one brother, and Mark's side of the family descends from the other brother. It was his personal family connection to this organization that sparked Mark's interest in learning more about his own cultural identity.

When Mark was in his mid-to-late teens, he had a lot of questions and felt confused about who he was. When he learned that he shared his last name with the founders of AIM, he read about the organization and learned about its occupation of the town of Wounded Knee, South Dakota, on the Pine Ridge Indian Reservation. Learning about his personal connection to this historic event made him want to know even more about his Native side.

"It was like peeling an onion, removing one layer at a time, only to find new challenges or questions," remembers Mark. "Learning from my elders gave me a whole new way

Mark Bellcourt and his students at a Mayan site in Akumal, Mexico.

of looking at the world and helped me make sense out of my experiences."

Mark believes children should never be a part of something that they don't really believe in just because they want to fit in. Long ago, Native Americans had to give up their values and way of life because the white people decided their way of life was better. He says it's important to hold to your values and ideas and to slip yourself into the world in a way that doesn't make you compromise them.

In Mark's view, we all choose how we deal with our problems. We can choose to blame others, hate ourselves, or use alcohol and drugs to numb our pain, or we can look upon our challenging experiences as learned lessons and get on with life.

Mark Bellcourt and his students near Hasting, New Zealand, during a class on Indigenous environmental knowledge.

"Everything that happened to me has led me to where I am today—the good, bad, and the ugly," he says. "My advice to kids is to not let the bad things keep you down. Don't be afraid of making mistakes. Bad things happen to us all."

During a recent session of a leadership class that he teaches, Mark and his students were discussing how technology has changed the ways we communicate with each other. One student wished he could just talk to his friends instead of texting all the time. Mark asked whether he would be willing to give up his phone and engage in a more direct conversation. He said, "No, I like the personal conversation, but it is just easier to say things without looking them in the face."

"I think technology is wonderful and enables us to do so much more," Mark says. "However, it also allows us to become faceless and avoid responsibility."

Mark Bellcourt

He feels the world has been sliding into a deep hole of greed and destruction. Rather than valuing human diversity, too many people of influence are encouraging division. He also believes that Mother Earth is being stripped of her resources.

"This is the first generation that is leaving the world in a worse place for future generations," he says. "But we are not responsible for the world. We can only be responsible for our part in the world. We should all strive to live better lives."

Bert Crowfoot

SIKSIKA NATION ELDER

Bert Crowfoot is an elder from the Siksika Nation who has the honor of having two First Nation names. His Siksika name is Kiyo Sta'ah, or "Bear Ghost." His Kwakwaka'wakw name is Gayutalas, or "Always Giving." He was honored with his second name when he was adopted by the Kwakwaka'wakw and their chief, Adam Dick.

Bert was born in 1953 in Gleichen, which is located in southern Alberta, Canada. He's half Blackfoot and is from the Siksika reserve. The Siksika are part of the Blackfoot Confederacy and speak the Blackfoot language, which is also known as Siksika. Bert is also a descendant of the Saulteaux, or Plains Ojibway, people from the Keys reserve near Kamsack, Saskatchewan. He is the great-great-grandson of the legendary Blackfoot chief Crowfoot and was named Bear Ghost after him. In 1877 Chief Crowfoot signed the important peace agreement Treaty 7 between the British government and a group of Canada's First Nations. In this treaty the Blackfoot agreed to live on a specifically designated area of land called a reserve.

Bert grew up and lived on a farm on the reserve. He has nine siblings and is the third oldest in the family as well as the oldest boy. His parents, Cecil and Frances Crowfoot, were Mormons.

His parents greatly influenced him when he was growing up. "They taught me to be proud of who I am and to be self-sufficient," says Bert. An example of this is the way Bert was taught to drive a tractor. When Bert was eight years old, his father set him up on the seat and told him to "keep the wheel in the rut." After seeing that Bert could handle it, Bert's father just jumped off the tractor and let Bert drive.

Bert kept to himself most of the time and had no close relationships with anyone his age. When he was twelve years old he got his first job on a neigh-

Bert Crowfoot

bor's farm, where he made twelve dollars a day.

When he was growing up on the reserve, his family was a little better off than most others because his father was a successful farmer. However, his parents worried about their children growing up around the poverty, drugs, and alcohol abuse that were part of life on the reserve. They thought the best thing they could do for their children was to enroll them in a special program offered by the Mormon Church for Indian children. The program placed Indian children in the homes of white families for the length of the school year. This made it possible for Indian children to attend schools off the reserve. The children went back to their homes for the summer.

When he was twelve years old and in the eighth grade, Bert's parents enrolled him in the Mormon Church's program, and he went to live with a white family in Calgary. He lived with them and attended school there for a year. He then moved to Edmonton and lived with a new family for his final four years of school.

Bert believes that his family really benefited from the program. His siblings have twenty-two college degrees among them and are very successful. Even though Bert went to the university, he is the only family member without a degree. He attended college in Utah at Brigham Young University (BYU) and was a student in their premedical program for the first year. In his second year he switched his major to physical education and recreation, but soon even those plans changed.

He met his wife, Linda Franklin, a Navajo from Arizona, at BYU. They married in 1974 and have two children, Sandra and Bradley, who are now grown.

During his time at the university, Bert worked as a silversmith and made turquoise jewelry. After three and a half years, he decided to take a year off from school and find a job to pay off some of his bills. It was hard to make a living as a silversmith since the income was not steady. He'd make a piece of jewelry, sell it, live on that money for a while, and then start all over again. Since he needed a more regular income, he decided to look elsewhere for work.

In 1977 Bert got his start in media work by writing freelance sports stories for a local Indian newspaper, *The Native People*. One thing led to another, and pretty soon Bert was learning the ins and outs of putting together and running a newspaper. He eventually worked his way up to be the publisher of the newspaper.

Bert's newspaper was part of the Alberta Native Communications Society, but after they lost their funding in 1982, Bert started the Aboriginal Multi-Media Society of Alberta (AMMSA) in 1983. AMMSA now has revenue of three million dollars a year and is the largest Aboriginal media outlet in Canada.

Bert now owns five newspapers and a radio station and is known as a leader in Aboriginal communications in North America. He is the publisher of the Aboriginal newspapers *Alberta Sweetgrass, Saskatchewan Sage, BC Raven's Eye,* and *Ontario Birchbark,* as well as *Windspeaker,* a national magazine covering issues in the Aboriginal community. Bert's also the General Manager of CFWE-FM, which is Alberta's first Aboriginal-owned radio network. CFWE reaches an audience of more than one hundred thousand listeners, most of whom are Aboriginal people living in rural communities throughout Alberta.

Bert has also expanded his media work to television and is the producer of the four-part documentary series aired on Canada's OMNI network, *Quest of Buffalo Spirit.*

"I had earlier asked the Creator, the grandfathers, and the grandmothers if I was doing the right thing with *Buffalo Spirit*," says Bert. "There was much confusion out in Indian Country regarding Indian spirituality and culture. The answer I received was that *Buffalo Spirit* was necessary to inform, educate, and create discussion regarding our cultural and spiritual way of life."

Bert has been instrumental in establishing several media industry associations, including the National Aboriginal Communications Society, the Alberta Magazine Publishers Association, and the Western Association of Aboriginal Broadcasters.

In 2006 Bert was inducted into the Dreamspeakers Film Festival Walk of Honour in the communications and multimedia category. This award is a tribute to Aboriginal people who have been at the forefront of the film industry. They are recognized for their efforts to foster understanding of the artistic expressions, cultures, languages, and traditions of Aboriginal people in Canada. He was named one of Alberta's

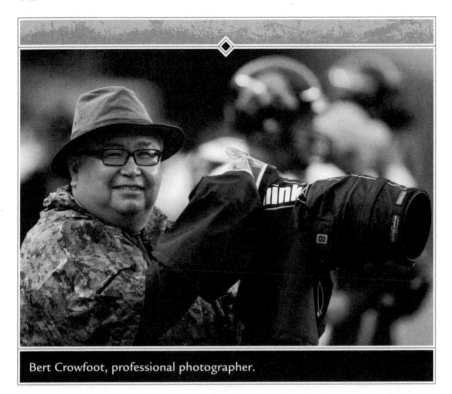

Bert Crowfoot, professional photographer.

50 Most Influential People by *Alberta Venture* magazine in 2004, and in 2005 he was awarded the Lifetime Achievement Award by the Tribal Chiefs Institute. In Alberta's centennial celebration he was picked as one of the one hundred entrepreneurs who helped build the region and make it what it is today.

In 2008, when Bert was adopted by the Kwakwa̱ka'wakw Nation of northern Vancouver Island, British Columbia, he was given his second name, Gayutalas, which means "always giving." The adoption ceremony took place at a potlatch, which is a gathering of people where gifts are given away and spiritual ceremonies take place. For most people, wealth and status are determined by how much you have, but the Kwakwa̱ka'wakw are different. For them, wealth is determined by how much you give away.

Even as busy as he is with his business endeavors, Bert still lives with a strong sense of who he is and where he's come from. He does beadwork and has a woodworking shop. He makes cradleboards, which were once used by First Nations and Native American women to carry their babies on their backs while going about their daily work.

Bert hunts, practices target shooting, and has made powwow dance outfits and danced the Men's Fancy Dance at many powwows in his earlier years. His paintings and bronze statues have made him one of the most successful First Nations fine artists in Alberta. In addition, because Bert played football and other sports in school, he wanted to coach team sports. He started out coaching his sister's basketball team as a young man, and later on he coached his daughter's teams. His softball and basketball teams had many wins and even went to championship competitions. He coached the Alberta women's softball team in the 1993 Canada Summer Games and is a nationally recognized softball coach. He retired from coaching in 2007.

Bert is also well known for his photography and has won many awards for his photos. He began studying photography in high school and used the skills he learned to take journalistic photos for a newspaper in 1977. Since then, Bert has received many awards for his sports and news photography from the Native American Journalists Association.

Over the course of his career, Bert has had four photo exhibitions. He has an intuitive eye and can size up a scene and decide how to portray it in the best light. He is best known for his photographs of dancers, taken at powwows across the country. Having been a dancer, Bert knows when to snap each picture. "I know when a dancer's going to do a certain thing," he explains.

He takes photos at ten to fifteen powwows a year. Many dancers have learned to trust him and let him take their portraits or action shots. They know that he will be respectful of the dance as well as the dancer and that he tries to capture the ceremony within the dance.

Because of everything he's accomplished, Bert is a respected elder of his tribe. He believes that all nations should have their elders' words and messages recorded in their own voices in order to preserve their knowledge. For his own contribution, Bert leads workshops as a way to pass down what he has learned in his lifetime. He teaches young people using both sports psychology and Indian spirituality. As he explains, "You have to talk *with* kids, not *at* them."

He believes it's important to teach young people to have a good attitude. His sports philosophy comes into play when he talks about the ten qualities of a winner. He teaches that the qualities of a winner are spiritual in nature and that the spiritual protectors of these qualities are the wolf, buffalo, eagle, and bear.

One of his favorite philosophies was given to him by a fifteen-year-old player before a game. The players each had to bring in a motivational saying to inspire the team. One girl's saying was, "Don't let winning go to your head or losing go to your heart!" Bert remembers that saying wherever he goes and uses it in everything he does; this is exactly what he tries to pass on to others.

"There are three types of people," says Bert, "winners, losers, and spectators. Winners are in the game and don't care what other people think about them, only what they think of themselves. Losers are in the game but don't have the right attitude. Spectators aren't even in the game. They sit on the sidelines and are critical of those in the game."

Bert Crowfoot is an elder who cares about future generations. If there is one lesson he wants to teach young people, it is the importance of getting to know themselves. When you spend time really learning who you are—from exploring your heritage to discovering and honing your own skills and

Bert Crowfoot using a large camera lens to get the perfect photo.

talents—you also learn to believe in yourself. And for Bert, believing in yourself is the key to always performing your best and being successful.

Louva Dahozy

NAVAJO ELDER

Whatever you do, stay in school. Learn all you can. Go to college and come home and make something out of yourself." Eighty-four-year-old Louva McCabe Dahozy has preached those words to young people, especially her children and grandchildren, for many years.

"I truly believe in education," says Louva. When she was five years old, her mother took her to boarding school in a wagon. Her mother said, "There is the school you wanted to go to. Go over there and start school." Not knowing that it was necessary, she left Louva there without giving anyone Louva's personal information, not even her name. When the teacher asked Louva her name, she answered in Navajo because she didn't have an English name. Someone at the school knew Louva's family, so the school gave her the name "Louva McCabe." But McCabe was her grandfather's last name.

Louva was born near Flagstaff, Arizona, on the western end of the Navajo reservation. The family was poor and lived in a hogan, which is a one-room Navajo dwelling where an entire family would cook, eat, and sleep. Even as a child Louva wanted to get away from that kind of life. She was determined to stay in school and get an education even if it meant leaving her family, living at the boarding school, and staying in a dormitory for the entire nine-month school term. One good thing came out of her having to stay at the school: she learned to roller skate and became very good at it.

Louva Dahozy

Every September, Louva would saddle up her horse and ride forty miles to return to the boarding school. If she wanted to go to school, she had to go by herself because there was no one to take her. Her mother was single and had to take care of one thousand head of cattle and sheep. She had no time to transport children. All of the children helped their mother with the chores—especially Louva, who was the oldest—but Louva was determined to get an education. She didn't want to have to take care of cattle and sheep for the rest of her life.

Life was hard at school, and she had to put up with bullying. "I grew up with nothing: no money, no nice clothes, and no love," she says. "The food was bad and there was not enough; all the students wore the same kind of clothes and the girls all had the same haircuts. We were beaten if we spoke Navajo." Despite the mistreatment and having to live at the school, Louva knew that education was the key to improving her life.

While attending high school, Louva planned to continue her education, but World War II broke out and the boarding school she attended was closed down and converted into internment camps for Japanese citizens. She had no one to turn to for help, so she had to get a job.

Even though she had to work, it was always Louva's goal to further her education. She attended school as much as possible when she could find a school near the reservation. During the summers she would go into Flagstaff to look for work. One summer, a girlfriend who lived in town helped her get a job working for two white families. She did housecleaning and cooking. "It helped me to learn to speak better English," she says. Louva eventually managed to graduate from Tuba City High School in Tuba City, Arizona.

When Louva was a teenager, she had a number of boyfriends. "I was careful not to make a fool of myself and made sure I selected the right man to marry." The right man turned out to be Wilson Dahozy, a Navajo who grew up on the reservation about two hundred miles from Louva's birthplace. He served in the US Army Air Force in World War II and was honorably discharged. When Louva met him he was working in an army depot as a heavy equipment operator and truck driver. After they married they moved to Parker, Arizona, near the reservation of the Colorado River Indian Tribes and about 470 miles away from the Navajo reservation. The Bureau of Indian Affairs gave them 160 acres of land to farm for as long as they wished. They grew cotton, alfalfa, watermelons, and cantaloupes.

Louva and Wilson raised their three daughters and two sons on their farm. "We raised our children the best way we knew how, by giving them responsibility, and we taught them to garden so they would have the right food to eat." The family attended church on a regular basis because they believed that teaching their children spirituality was important.

While Louva was living in Parker, extension agents from the University of Arizona (who typically work in rural areas) provided her with many educational opportunities. She learned how to care for elders and cook nutritious foods. She also learned how to sew clothes and become self-sufficient. In addition, she was taught how to raise different animals, including ducks, chickens, rabbits, sheep, and milk cows. For the next forty years Louva passed on this knowledge to parents and children through 4-H programs, all on a volunteer basis.

After living in Parker for fifteen years, Louva developed a bad case of asthma from breathing the dust and pollen that were stirred up when fields were plowed and planted. Her doctor recommended that she move to a higher altitude, so the family packed up all its belongings and moved to Fort Defiance, Arizona, near the New Mexico border.

In 1970 Louva helped start the North American Indian Women's Association. It was formed to support the health and education of Native women, to increase awareness of Indian cultures, and to encourage the betterment of home, family life, and community. Both Canada's First Nations and American Indians are qualified to belong. The group obtained funding from the United States Congress to help resolve problems on reservations. Louva was elected the first national membership chairwoman of the association.

Louva also helped set up the National Indian Council on Aging and put together the Navajo Nation Council on Aging. She wrote the first Navajo cookbook of recipes that include both government commodity food and natural Native foods. She has conducted studies proving that diets based on traditional Navajo foods are healthier and have a higher nutritional content than modern diets packed with fat, sugar, and salt.

To this day, she conducts food demonstrations at schools and colleges and teaches about nutrition and the benefits of eating healthy food. She tells people about the Navajo in the past who were strong and healthy from eating the wild plants they gathered and the animals they hunted. She explains how people gathered wild grass seeds for grain and ground the corn that they grew.

Through her work with 4-H, Louva has spent a lifetime helping people lead healthy lives. She has taught hundreds of young people about livestock and home economics. Her dedication was recognized in 1994 when she received a Lifetime Award from the University of Arizona's College of Agriculture and Life Sciences.

Louva is now a grandmother, and her advice to her grandchildren and young people everywhere is still the same as it was to her own children: "Stay in school." She is proud that as a mother and grandmother she taught her children and grandchildren as much as she could about Navajo life, but also taught them about the white man's culture they interacted with almost daily. Her children and grandchildren are nurses and teachers, and one holds a doctoral degree in education. Many are in leadership positions in the Navajo Nation. One of her grandsons has served his country with three tours in Iraq and Afghanistan.

When asked "What are your hopes for the future generation?" she replied, "I am hoping that our tribal government makes it a priority of how important it is to educate our children. They are our future generation. I hope the young people have a better life and learn what the outside world is doing and bring it back to our reservation and help us improve. We don't need to be on a food stamp program, a donated foods program, and free handouts, but to grow our own food and develop our own jobs. Also, to take care of our elders because they have information which we need to tap into in order to be successful people."

Speaking about her motivation for the work she's done throughout her life, Louva says, "I wanted to provide traditional and modern education for Navajo people, so they might have a better life."

Faith Davison

MOHEGAN ELDER

Faith Davison is an elder from the Mohegan Tribe of South Central Connecticut. When she retired in 2011 after serving fourteen years as the archivist and librarian of the Mohegan Tribe, the Mohegan Tribal Council of Elders named Faith a *nonner*, which means an elder female of respect. Before retiring, at the age of seventy, she established the Mohegan Library and Tribal Archives. The library and archives currently hold over 8,000 volumes, including both fiction and nonfiction works by Native American authors and books about Native American tribes, particularly those of the Northeast. Faith has also published and contributed to a variety of scholarly publications on the topic of Mohegan history and helped develop courses about the Mohegan Tribe for use in Connecticut public schools.

Faith was born in New London, Connecticut, in 1940, just before World War II. She has three younger sisters. Her parents worked hard to provide for their family, and Faith appreciates the good job they did raising her and her sisters.

Her mother, Virginia Hope Sword Damon, was very smart and graduated from West Warwick High in Rhode Island when she was sixteen years old. After graduating from high school, Faith's mother attended Johnson & Wales University to learn about business machines and bookkeeping.

Left to right: Christine Ann, Cheryl Inez, and Faith Marie, the three oldest Damon girls.

Faith's father, Harland Le Roy Damon, never had the chance to finish high school. When Harland was only four- teen, his father deserted the family and he had to quit school and get a job to help his mother. They lived at the head of the Niantic River, so Harland was able to get a job on a Mer- ritt-Chapman & Scott dredge, a boat that is fitted with equip- ment used to deepen channels in rivers. The job required him to travel up and down the east coast of the United States. Although he was only fourteen, he worked very hard because he had a mother and sister to help provide for.

Faith grew up in the village of Niantic, Connecticut, right beside the water of the Long Island Sound. She eventually raised her children there too. It was a small village then, with only eight grades at Niantic Center School. Faith enjoyed learning, and she was reading long before she began school. To give an idea of just how small the school was, there were fewer than thirty students in each grade from first through sixth grades. The seventh and eighth grades were a little larger, as the local kids were joined by other students from a nearby town, but there was still only one classroom for each grade.

Faith's very best friend was Rosemarie (whom she called Ree), the daughter of her father's work supervisor, who lived one street over from Faith's family. Today Rosemarie lives in Warren, Rhode Island, and they still talk on the phone and write letters to each other.

One of Faith's favorite childhood memories is of the party boat that Ree's father ran on the Niantic River during the summers for a little side income. He would charge vacationing city folks to take them fishing for the day.

"Ree and I would swamp out the boat and load the bait in," she says. "Sometimes we'd even bait the hooks for the more squeamish fellows. Some of these men would even take a hotel room for the weekend so they could go out fishing both days."

Faith says that after a successful day out fishing, the city folk would pose at the dock for pictures with their catch. Unless they had a really large fish for the taxidermist, they weren't interested in keeping them. Ree's father was a good businessman, so he knew just what to do with all the unwanted fish.

"Ree's father would take the freshly caught but unwanted fish around to the hotel's kitchen door and sell them," she says. "We all would get a good laugh about how city folks liked to pay for fish twice."

Drawing, painting, and reading were some of Faith's favorite things to do when she was growing up. She also made fishing lures and sold them to vacationing fishermen. Another favorite pastime was riding bikes all over town—sometimes even with her .22-caliber rifle slung over her back.

"I think that if you saw a nine-year-old girl riding a bike and carrying a .22 rifle today, she'd be turned in to children's services and her parents would probably be arrested," says Faith. "But back then we could go shooting at an old gravel river bank or at the dump without any interference."

Faith says the kids she grew up with all carried jackknives. Some of the kids kept knives strapped to their ankles to use if they got tangled in the rope and were swept overboard from a fishing boat while hauling in lobster pots, or if they had to walk their traplines and cut something loose. She never saw a knife pulled in anger during her childhood. Everyone she knew considered a knife to be just another tool.

Faith considers her childhood typical. She and her friends jumped rope and played marbles and hopscotch. She also liked to sew clothes for her sisters' dolls, even though she didn't like to play with dolls herself. Faith learned to embroider, but it wasn't until she was fifty-seven years old that she taught herself to crochet using a book from the children's section of the library.

She loved spending school holidays with her Grandfather Sword, who was an inventor. She also very much enjoyed spending weekends with her mother's mother, whom they called "Ma." Ma lived on Jordan Cove, near New London, Connecticut.

"Ma and I would go crabbing in late summer," Faith says. "After they were all boiled up, we'd sit at the table under the open boathouse roof by Jordan Cove and pick crabmeat until they were all cleaned and we had enough meat for a big salad. Often she'd have a little juice-glass of beer to sip while we worked, and I would have Moxie (the official soft drink of Maine). In late summer, the yellow jackets would be even more aggressive than usual. Ma always said that the little glass of beer, into which they would dive and drown, would let them 'die happy' and they would leave the crabmeat and shells alone. She was right."

Faith remembers that Ma loved to be driven to all kinds of places and loved to dine out, but most of all she loved picking blueberries. All the women in Faith's family would come up to Mohegan and pick blueberries all day. Both of her mother's parents were fond of children and enjoyed their company, but her father's parents just tolerated them. Both sets of grandparents were divorced, so the children had four separate households they could visit.

Faith grew up during the height of World War II. Her family had ration books for buying groceries and meatless weeks like everyone else in the country. Because they lived along the coastline, fishermen depended upon regular weather forecasts, but during the war the forecasts were stopped. It was thought that German submarines might intercept the information and use it to their advantage. For his war effort, Faith's father joined the Merchant Marine. With his wife's help, he learned the navigation portion of the exam and eventually earned his master's Merchant Marine papers.

"During his service, he sailed Liberty ships across the Atlantic," Faith says. "He was delivering goods to our allies who were in danger of starving." Sometimes Faith's father would be away for three or four months.

Faith's mother stayed home and tended a one-acre garden in which she grew everything they could eat or preserve to feed them throughout the winter. She was the keeper of the coal furnace, too. She always knew how to bank the coal in the evening so the family could have a quick fire when they woke up. Faith's mother taught Red Cross courses and also knitted wool caps for servicemen to wear inside their helmets and mittens to keep their hands warm.

Faith's family lived around the corner from the National Guard camp. Often the family's rooster would be up before the National Guard bugler who played reveille every morning. Faith remembers watching the new men arrive to begin their training and later watching them parade down to the train station when their training was complete.

The camp had block wardens, whose job was to make certain that everyone living on or near the base camp used blackout curtains at night. No chances were taken that the pilot of

Faith Davison with Paul Grant-Costa on a panel representing the Yale Indian Papers Project at the fourth annual meeting of the Native American and Indigenous Studies Association.

an enemy plane could spot the area at night. If a family had any light showing, their warden would not be happy.

After the war was over, Faith's father left the Merchant Marines, and in 1948 he started a business to support his family. He sold International Harvester tractors and lawn mowers. He also sharpened mower blades, skates, and saws, and he could pick a lock when people locked themselves out of their homes. Faith's mother was the bookkeeper for the business and also made keys. During slow times, Faith's father would do carpentry and also create custom gun stocks. He taught her how to sharpen tools, and she learned to love working with her hands.

Faith's mother always knew that her daughter had good common sense and would stay out of trouble, so she didn't have very many rules for her daughter to follow. Her intuition was correct. Faith fished, crabbed, scalloped, mowed lawns, and shoveled snow for pocket money. She also pumped gas and sold live bait. Her first official job was at a drugstore when she was sixteen years old. In the summer, she pumped gas and worked as a waitress in a little restaurant called the Sweden House. She had her first car before she was sixteen; it had been her grandfather's.

Faith was a good student, but she found school to be boring. She would much rather have been outdoors or out on the water reading a book than sitting in a classroom. But even though she was bored, she studied and graduated from high school with honors.

Eventually Faith married and started a family. She began taking college courses but only took one course every semester. She really didn't think about getting a degree because she was too busy raising children, working, and keeping house. But once her kids were grown, she had the opportunity to go to school full-time. She had accumulated 120 credits over the years from the community college and the University of Connecticut, so her college advisor said that she should try entering college as a junior at a four-year school. Faith was admitted into Connecticut College on an academic scholarship. She and her youngest son both got their undergraduate degrees in 1986! His was in finance and hers was in anthropology.

Faith then went to work for Mystic Seaport, the nation's leading maritime museum, but planned to go back to school. In 1994, she decided to get a master's degree in library and information studies. The closest school that offered this degree was the University of Rhode Island. Even though she lived in the state of Connecticut at the time, she was admitted on an academic scholarship to the University of Rhode Island. When the school's administration found out that she wouldn't borrow money for her living expenses, they made her a graduate assistant and the head of a computer lab and paid her a stipend. She was learning just ahead of the people she was teaching. She was able to earn her Master of Library and Information Studies degree in a year and a half.

Faith always had an inquisitive mind and is a jack-of-all-trades. She enjoyed reading and believes it helped get her where she is today. She always asked questions about anything she didn't understand. She took advantage of every opportunity to learn how to use tools or operate equipment, both at home and at work. Faith can drive a tractor and a forklift. She can sail, fly a biplane, run a motorboat, and cut down a tree safely. She does landscape gardening and has even written a book on how to make medicines using only plants native to the area where she lives. Faith plays keyboard, she knows how to prepare freshly killed deer, chicken, or fish for cooking, and she has used ditch-digging dynamite to blow up tree stumps. She's even made fireworks!

"We had lots of unscheduled, unsupervised time where we could test our limits, physically and mentally," says Faith about her childhood. "How long could you stay under water or drive a small car on an iced-over pond? Seeing if you can find a specimen to add to your butterfly collection, or a new stamp, or identifying bones found in the woods. Dreaming of what it was like before the settlers came and one had to know how to live in order to survive."

Faith learned the value of hard work. She has never had a car or boat payment and she has always paid her houses off ahead of time. She feels that if you're going to throw money around, you should use it to travel. It's a wide world filled with lots of things to see and learn. Faith retired when she was seventy, and now she's so busy she wonders how she ever found the time to go to work.

Her advice for children and young adults is to read everything they can and to set realistic goals. Faith points out that you never know when something you read will come in handy in the future. Another important bit of advice she gives kids is to listen to your folks. Her grandfather once told her that as she got older, *he* would get smarter.

"And he was right," says Faith. "Some of the things I learned from him still come in handy. One important thing he taught me is to look at a situation from every possible angle before you start to solve it."

Faith says that keeping an open mind and staying in school is important. She doesn't believe that people can get a job to support a family on just a high school education anymore. She knows that if she had gone to college right after high school, she probably would have doubled her earning power. However, she says it's important to find a field you like and make that your job, even if it doesn't pay as much as something you don't like.

Faith goes on to remind children to know their surroundings, their family, and their history. "Live so that when people speak of you after you pass away, you will gladden their hearts," she says. "Give back to the community from where you came. Never do anything to shame the people who care for you. There are fewer than two thousand people in my tribe, and this is a nation of over three hundred million people. I conduct myself courteously when meeting people, and I am pleasant and mannerly in conversation. I know that I might be the only Mohegan that someone will meet and that they will judge my people by my behavior."

She hopes that this generation's children will not allow themselves to be lured by easy money or an easy life. She also believes that the only hope for our nation is in diplomacy. "We cannot afford another war," says Faith. "I hope that children learn several languages to more easily understand cultural differences. I hope that children can live on high ground so that the sea will not cover their land. I hope that children will work together for the greater good of all. Be smart, be honest. Thrive."

Aboriginal Multi-Media Society of Alberta (AMMSA). The Aboriginal Multi-Media Society was formed in 1983 to serve the communication needs of Aboriginal people across Canada. The association provides training, support, and encouragement to any Aboriginal group starting its own communications facility.

Anishinaabe. Anishinaabe means "first or original peoples." It refers to the Ojibwe, (Ojibwa, Ojibway), Odawa, and Algonquin (Algonkin) peoples. These tribes share closely related Algonquian languages.

Anthropology. Anthropology is the study of humanity that focuses on human culture and human development.

Comanche. Historically, the Comanche tribe lived in parts of New Mexico, Arizona, Texas, Oklahoma, and Kansas. They were one of the first tribes to acquire horses from Spanish explorers, and they soon became known as expert horsemen and horse breeders. They are a federally recognized tribe, now located in Oklahoma, with a tribal enrollment of 15,191.

Doctorate of letters. In the United States, a doctorate of letters is an honorary degree given by universities to individuals in recognition of their accomplishments in the field of humanities or for their charitable work.

Ferryboat. A ferryboat is a boat or ship that carries people, vehicles, and/or goods across a body of water, especially over a relatively short distance or as a regular service.

First Nation. First Nation tribes are Aboriginal people of Canada who are not Métis or Inuit. There are approximately

630 First Nation tribes or bands with a total population of 700,000 people.

Graduate assistant. A graduate assistant is a person who helps a professor at a college or university, usually by teaching or doing research. Graduate assistants have typically already earned bachelor's degrees and are working on advanced degrees during their assistantships.

Gwich'in. The Gwich'in are a First Nation band of 150 people who live above the Arctic Circle. Their name means "One Who Dwells." The Gwich'in are also known as "the Caribou People" and subsist on Porcupine caribou.

Homestead. A homestead is a place where a person or family makes their home. A homestead includes the house, land, and all other buildings. In the Homestead Act of 1862, the US government gave settlers tracts of public land to develop into farms.

Hudson Bay Company middleman. A Hudson Bay Company middleman was a First Nation man who gathered fur hides from First Nation trappers and delivered them to the Hudson Bay Company forts along Canada's Hudson Bay. The middleman traded the hides for colorful beads, cooking pots, blankets, and guns. The middleman then returned to the First Nations bands with the traded supplies.

Infantryman. An infantryman is a member of the US Army Infantry. This branch of an army is known as its backbone. The infantrymen are also referred to as foot soldiers because they are soldiers who train to fight on foot, face-to-face against enemy ground forces.

Inuit. The Inuit are Aboriginal people living in the Arctic regions of Canada, Greenland, Russia, and the United States. Groups of Inuit people living across these areas share cultural similarities. The Canadian Constitution Act of 1982 declared the Inuit people living in Canada as a separate group that is not classified as either First Nation or Métis.

Jackknife. A jackknife is a knife that folds. It has one or more blades that fit inside the knife handle.

Jack-of-all-trades. A jack-of-all-trades is a person who has many skills.

Jingle Dress Dance. Originating with the Ojibwe, the Jingle Dress Dance is now incorporated into the dress and dance of other tribes. The Ojibwe believe the dress and dance are for healing. The dress worn in the dance has many rows of metal cones sewed onto it. As the dancer moves, the cones make a jingling sound.

Kwakwa̱ka'wakw Nation. The Kwakwa̱ka'wakw Nation are Indigenous people who live in British Columbia, northern Vancouver Island, and some mainland areas. Today they are organized into thirteen political bands, each with its own government. Only 5 percent, or about 250 people, speak the Kwak'wala language.

Liberty ships. Liberty ships were inexpensive, easy-to-construct cargo ships built in large numbers by the United States for use during World War II. These ships could carry substantial amounts of cargo, up to nine thousand tons, in addition to numerous tanks, locomotives, and airplanes.

Men's Fancy Dance. The Men's Fancy Dance is a strenuous, athletic dance created by the Ponca tribe in the 1920s and 1930s. It's now danced by people of many different tribes at most powwows. The regalia, or ceremonial dress, worn for the dance is brightly colored and adorned with feathers and ribbons that represent the rainbow spirits. The dance is fast-paced and involves a lot of jumping and twirling, with one goal being to keep the feathers and ribbons of the regalia in motion at all times. Fancy dancers must train extensively for strength, agility, and endurance.

Merchant Marine. The Merchant Marine is a fleet of commercial ships owned by US civilians. The US government operates some of these ships, and private shipping companies operate others. The ships carry passengers and cargo through the passable bodies of water of the United States. During a war, the ships of the Merchant Marine help the US Navy by delivering troops and supplies where needed.

Métis. The Métis are a Canadian Aboriginal group of people whose ancestry is traced to marriages between Aboriginal women and European men. The Métis are a distinct Aboriginal group who are not considered either First Nation or Inuit.

North West Rebellion. The North West Rebellion of 1885, also known as the Métis Resistance, occurred when the Métis protested the government takeover of Batoche, a settlement that the Métis had established in Saskatchewan in 1872. The Canadian government planned on forcing out the Métis to make room for white settlers. A small band of three hundred Métis and other Aboriginal people fought against a force of eight hundred government troops. After four days of fierce fighting, the Métis and Aboriginal troops surrendered.

Moxie. Moxie is a soft drink that was originally marketed as a nerve tonic in the 1870s and was advertised as a cure for "nervousness." It has been a tradition in the New England states since 1884. It's the oldest continually produced soft drink in the United States.

National Guard. The National Guard is a branch of the United States Army. It consists primarily of civilians who serve their state and community on a part-time basis. They attend training camp one weekend each month and two weeks during the summer. The governor of each state can call the National Guard into active duty during local or statewide emergencies, including earthquakes, fires, and storms. In addition, the president of the United States can activate National Guard units during a time of war.

Ojibwe. The Ojibwe people (whose name is also spelled Ojibwa or Ojibway, and who are also known as the Chippewa) live in both Canada and the United States. They are the second largest First Nation group in Canada and the fourth largest Native American tribe in the United States.

The Order of Canada. The Order of Canada is the country's highest honor for lifetime achievement. It is awarded to Canadian citizens who have contributed significantly to their community and nation. People who have received the Order of Canada represent a variety of backgrounds and careers and include artists, business people, doctors, educators, and scientists.

Potlatch. A traditional potlatch is a ceremony of the cultures of the Northwest Coast First Nation and American Indian tribes. A potlatch includes songs, dances, and rituals. One of the rituals is the giving away of material goods. By giving items away, a family or an individual can gain status in the tribe. This is also a way of distributing surplus wealth among members.

Quonset hut. With a design based on the British Nissen hut, a Quonset hut is a lightweight structure made of prefabricated metal with a semicircular shape.

Reserve. A "reserve" is the Canadian term for a government-owned tract of land that is set aside for use by a First Nation band for their benefit. The Indian Act of 1876 gave the Canadian government authority to regulate land reserved for Aboriginal people. The Indian Act also defined who was an Indian (and who was not), something that could not be challenged in a court of law.

Reveille. Reveille is a bugle or trumpet call associated with the military. It is traditionally played at sunrise to wake military troops.

Silversmith. A silversmith is a person who creates objects from silver, such as jewelry, dishes, or flatware.

Sobriety. Sobriety is the continual non-use of alcohol or mind-altering drugs.

Spitfire airplane. A spitfire was a single-seat airplane that was built for war missions. It was expected to last for only one hundred missions.

Taxidermist. A taxidermist is a person who prepares, stuffs, and mounts the skins of dead animals, birds, and fish in such a way that they appear to be alive.

Treaty 7. Treaty 7, signed in 1877, is one of the eleven numbered treaties signed between Blackfoot First Nation tribes and Queen Victoria of England. This treaty gave the Blackfoot First Nation tribes tracts of land called reserves, promised them payments from the queen, and gave them continued hunting and trapping rights on the reserve. In exchange, the Blackfoot First Nation tribes gave up their rights to their traditional territories.

Tr'ondëk Hwëch'in First Nation. The Tr'ondëk Hwëch'in First Nation Band lives along the Yukon River in the area in and around Dawson City, Canada. They are descendants of the Hän-speaking people who traded with other First Nation people in the area. In 1991 the Tr'ondëk Hwëch'in started negotiations with the Canadian government for legal claim to their land. In 1998 the final agreement was signed.

Voyageur. "Voyageur" is a French word that means "traveler." A voyageur was a person who was employed by a fur-trading company to transport goods during the 1700s and 1800s. They carried supplies to fur trappers to trade for furs. These brave, strong men traveled into the interior of Canada by canoe and hiked nearly impassable trails. There are many references to voyageurs in folklore and music.

World War II. In 1939, Germany (led by Adolph Hitler), Italy (led by Benito Mussolini), and Japan (led by Emperor Hirohito) formed a pact with the goal of taking over the world. They began attacking and taking over smaller countries. The United States, Great Britain, France, and Soviet Russia, along with Canada and eight other countries, formed an alliance and became known as the Allies.

By the time the war ended in 1945, over one hundred million people from thirty countries had served in the war. An estimated fifty to seventy-five million people, both military and civilian, died. Sixteen million Americans served during the war, and four hundred thousand died. The total number of deaths makes World War II the deadliest war in history.

Xwisten First Nation. The Xwisten First Nation is also known as the Bridge River Indian Band. The band is located in British Columbia, Canada, and is part of the St'át'mic culture. Hallmarks of the culture include the potlatch, clan names, mythology, and respect given to those who are wealthy and generous.

For more information about topics found in the LaDonna Harris chapter, visit:

Americans for Indian Opportunity: aio.org

Citizens Party: votecitizens.org

Comanche Nation: comanchenation.com

Common Cause: commoncause.org

National Women's Political Caucus: nwpc.org

For more information about topics in the Ernest Siva chapter, visit:

The Dorothy Ramon Learning Center: dorothyramon.org

Idyllwild Arts Academy and Summer Program: idyllwildarts.org

Morongo Band: morongonation.org

For more information about topics in the Jacqueline Guest chapter, visit:

Aboriginal World War II veterans: http://esask.uregina.ca/entry/aboriginal_peoples_and_the_world_wars.html

Indspire Award: newswire.ca/en/story/1053623/indspire-announces-2013-indspire-award-recipients

Métis: metisnation.ca

For more information about topics in the Percy Henry chapter, visit:

Assembly of First Nations: afn.ca/index.php/en

Council of Yukon First Nations: cyfn.ca

Takudh (Gwich'in First Nation language): ynlc.ca/languages/gw/gw.html

Top of the World Highway: northtoalaska.com/newsletters/winter2012/Alaska_Highway.aspx

Tr'ondëk Hwëch'in First Nation: cyfn.ca/ournationsthfn

Yukon First Nations Land Claims Settlement Act: http://laws-lois.justice.gc.ca/eng/acts/Y-2.3/page-1.html

For more information about topics in the Nella Heredia chapter, visit:

The Bureau of Indian Affairs: bia.gov/WhoWeAre/BIA/index.htm

Cahuilla Band of Indians: cahuillabandofindians.com

Pechanga Band of Luiseño Indians: pechanga-nsn.gov

Peon game: kumeyaay.info/games/peon_peone.html

For more information about topics in the Jim Northrup chapter, visit:

Anishinaabe/Ojibwe: ojibwe.org/home/about_anish.html

Cuban missile crisis: history.com/topics/cuban-missile-crisis

Fond du Lac Reservation: www.fdlrez.com

United States Marine Corps: marines.mil

Vietnam War: pbs.org/battlefieldvietnam/history/index.html

For more information about topics in the Judy Gingell chapter, visit:

Bill C-31: openparliament.ca/bills/41-1/C-31

Indian Act of 1876: firstpeoplesofcanada.com/fp_treaties/john_fp33_indianact.html

Tagish Kwan: kwanlindunculturalcentre.com/about-us/ourfirst-nation

Yukon Indian Women's Association: gov.yk.ca/news/09-247.html

Yukon Native Brotherhood: cyfn.ca/historylandclaims12

For more information about topics in the Christine Jack chapter, visit:

Pit house: wellpinit.org/pithouses

Residential schools: http://indigenousfoundations.arts.ubc.
ca/home/government-policy/the-residential-school-system.html

Xwisten First Nation: xwisten.ca/index.htm

aboriginalbc.com/xwisten-experience-tours

*For more information about topics in the Mark Bellcourt chapter,
visit:*

American Indian Movement: aimovement.org

Ojibwe: britannica.com/EBchecked/topic/426328/Ojibwa

*For more information about topics in the Bert Crowfoot chapter,
visit:*

Aboriginal Multi-Media Association: ammsa.com

Buffalo Spirit Communications Foundation: buffalospirit.org

Siksika Nation: siksikanation.com

Dreamspeakers Film Festival: dreamspeakers.org

First Nations: firstpeoplesofcanada.com/fp_treaties/fp_
treaties_treaty7.html

Potlatch: nativeamericannetroots.net/diary/631/the-potlatch

*For more information about topics in the Louva Dahozy chapter,
visit:*

4-H: 4-H.org

National Indian Council on Aging: nicoa.org

Navajo Nation: discovernavajo.com

North American Indian Women's Association: britannica.
com/EBchecked/topic/418880/North-American-Indian-
Womens-Association-NAIWA

Traditional Navajo foods: tribalconnections.org/health_
news/secondary_features/traditional.html

*For more information about topics in the Faith Davison chapter,
visit:*

Merchant Marine: www.usmma.edu/about/usmma-history

Mohegan Tribe: www.mohegan.nsn.us

National Guard: nationalguard.mil

K im Sigafus is an award-winning freelance writer and photographer from Illinois. An Ojibwe, she is enrolled in the White Earth Indian Reservation in northern Minnesota.

Journalistically, Kim spent ten years writing for newspapers in Wisconsin and Illinois. She had a three-year stint as editor of a small Iowa newspaper, where she won the McGregor/Marquette Chamber of Commerce Media Specialist Award; the Prairie du Chien, Wisconsin, Faith and Freedom Award; and the Lena D. Myers Award for her historic writing. As an author, she's written a children's book called *The Dress* and a walking-tour book on McGregor, Iowa. In 2011 she released *The Life and Times of the Ojibwa People* with writing partner Lyle Ernst. In 2012, Kim coauthored her first book for Book Publishing Company, *Native Writers: Voices of Power*, which won second place in the 2013 Fore-Word Review Book of the Year Award, was a finalist in the 2013 Next Generation Indie Book Awards for Native Writers, and was a finalist in the 2012 USA Best Book Awards in the Children's Non-Fiction category. She's also written for the yearly edition of *Photographer's Market*.

Kim moved to Freeport, Illinois, in 2012, where she lives with her beautiful cat, Kal, and her feisty Jack Russell Terrier, Animosh, which means "dog" in Ojibwe. Having been bitten by the theatrical bug in second grade, she enjoys singing and acting and performs in several shows a year.

L yle Ernst is a member of the Native American Coalition of the Quad Cities, based in Moline, Illinois. He is a freelance journalist and has contributed news stories, feature stories, and columns to Iowa newspapers, including the Cedar Rapids *Gazette*, the *Clayton County Reg-*

ister, the *Waukon Standard,* and in Wisconsin, the *Allamakee Journal* and the Prairie du Chien *Courier Press.*

Currently, Lyle is a freelance writer for the daily Illinois newspapers the *Moline Dispatch* and the *Rock Island Argus,* as well as for the weekly *Review.* Lyle has published articles in *Radish, Our Iowa,* and *Women's Edition* magazines. He has contributed essays to three books edited by Robert Wolf: *An American Mosaic, Heartland Portrait,* and *River Days: Stories from the Mississippi,* and also to *Make Hay While the Sun Shines,* edited by Jean Tennant.

He has written two books with his friend Kim Sigafus: *The Life and Times of the Ojibwa People* and *Native Writers: Voices of Power.*

Lyle lives in Davenport, Iowa, with his wife, Pat, and TT, an energetic doxie. His website is authorlyleernst.webs.com.

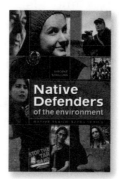
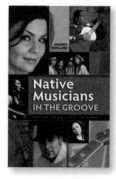
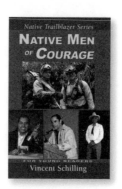